Birmingham Repertory Theatre Company
presents

Trips
By Sarah Woods

First Performance at The Door,
Birmingham Repertory Theatre
on 26 February 1999

SUPPORTED BY
THE NATIONAL LOTTERY
THROUGH
THE ARTS COUNCIL
OF ENGLAND

Providing Theatre for Birmingham

Paddy Irishman, Paddy Englishman and Paddy...?

By Declan Croghan

Thu 4 Feb - Sat 20 Feb

'What we have to do now is to focus our minds on how we are going to get ourselves out of this situation'.

Kevin and Anto are mates. They're getting by; earning a few spondoolicks, cooking enormous fry ups, avoiding the bad pint and trying desperately to understand women.

But last night a good turn turned bad, and now they've stumbled into something much bigger than both of them. The situation is exploding out of all control and their Irish past is about to come crashing in on their London lives.

Declan Croghan's hilarious black comedy looks at freedom and prejudice, heroism and cowardice and asks to whom we owe our true allegiances.

Director: Anthony Clark
Designer: Patrick Connellan
Lighting: Tim Mitchell

After Dark: Wed 17 Feb
(after the perf)

Trips

By Sarah Woods

Fri 26 Feb - Sat 20 Mar

'Have you ever wondered why you find a four and a half foot tall yellow cat more comforting than your own friends?'

What happens when you lose your focus in this dazzling new land of opportunity? Nik, John, Hayley, Dan and Glen are off on a night out; drugs, clubs and the fantastic twenty four hour garage. But tonight things are not quite going to plan.

Searching for love, excitement and one infallible business idea they are all about to encounter more than they ever thought possible. And what has Princess Anne got to

do with it all?.
Sarah Woods' bold, funny and technologically astonishing new play combines live performance with video to explore where we are now, and where we are all heading.

Director: Jeremy Raison
Designer: Kit Surrey

After Dark: 17 Mar
(after the perf)

Nightbus

By Peter Cann
Wed 24 Mar - Sat 3 Apr

'I'm not the kind of person things happen to.'

Meet Donna. She's a tour guide on one of those open-topped Birmingham Tour buses and she knows her city. The city of 1001 trades, of the Rotunda and Spaghetti Junction: the city with more parks than Paris, more miles of canal than Venice and less fun than Dudley, or so it seems. But Donna doesn't care. Hers is a safe life,

governed by electronic organisers, regular hours and familiar routes and routines.

But tonight, fate takes a hand in launching Donna into a bus-ride into weird and unfamiliar territory: into the twilight world below the flyovers: one of backstreet cosmetic surgeons and genetic engineers, of phoney traffic wardens, hotel receptionists, escaped chimpanzees, terrifying swimming instructors and crazy bargemen - all out to steal Donna's heart.

Using original, live music, five inventive performers will be brought together in this action

packed comic journey for all the family - beyond the outer margins of the city we know - or think we know.

NIGHTBUS is the first of this year's Rep Community Tours funded by the Sir Barry Jackson Trust

Director: Phil Tinline
Designer: Jens Cole

After Dark: Wed 31 Mar
(after the performance)

Feb 99 - June 99

'The largest and potentially most important space outside London dedicated exclusively to new work'
The Guardian Guide

Tickets: £9.00
Concs: £7.00
Standby: £5.00
(limited availability)
Mad to Miss Mondays:
£2.99, Under 26's

Produced in association with Soho Theatre Company

Perpetua

By Fraser Grace

Thu 15 Apr - Sat 8 May

'When a person feels betrayed by the law they trust in, they start to feel there is no way to do good 'cept by forcing themselves to do bad'

Are some lives worth more than others? The town of Pensacola, Florida is about to be set alight by the fiercest of battles. A struggle that pits the law of God against the law of the land, and the right to life against the right to choose.

On one side of the city stands May Lake abortion clinic, on the other the headquarters of the pro-life extremists Operation Freedom. At the centre of both organizations is a woman with a personal crusade. As the battle rages and the stakes get higher the two women are drawn closer, with potentially murderous consequences.

Fraser Grace's gripping new play challenges our deepest moral beliefs.

Director: Jonathan Lloyd
Designer: Timothy Meaker

All That Trouble That We Had

By Paul Lucas

Thu 13 May - Sat 5 Jun

'We're only good people gone slightly desperate'

When you're in despair no action seems too extreme. On one side of a bridge a daughter employs reckless measures to secure the return of her dead mother. On the other side a man reads *Heroes of Crime* and contemplates the craziest of schemes. And always in the background the distant sound of bodies splashing down from the bridge into the river.

But what part does the cheery, cigar smoking postmistress play? And who is the overweight salesman suddenly dropped into their lives? And are these bizarre happenings really chance, malice or destiny?

All That Trouble That We Had is a darkly comic and vivacious tale of wickedness on the margins of society celebrates the hopeless, the lonely and the unsuccessful, and explores our capricious ability to survive in vicious times.

Director: Anthony Clark

**After Dark: 6 Jun
(After the perf)**

In the Main House

No Such Thing...

**Theatre in the 80's
Sat 13 Mar**

Michael Billington, theatre critic for The Guardian, celebrates the ground-breaking theatre of the 1980's, joined by leading practitioners for a lively afternoon of show extracts and debate. This landmark event, which will include audience discussion, is the Birmingham Rep's contribution to the Towards the Millennium Festival of the 80's.

Performance: 2pm
Tickets: £5.00
Concs: £3.00

Trips
By Sarah Woods

CAST

Lisa Ellis Hayley

Karina Fernandez Nik

Karen Tomlin Ang

Simeon Defoe John

James Hillier Dan

Russell Mabey Glen

Director Jeremy Raison

Author/Assistant Director Sarah Woods

Designer Kit Surrey

Lighting Designer Symon Harner

Video Maker Rachel Davies

Animation Assistants Ben Davies, Jeremy Bass

Stage Manager Niki Ewen

Deputy Stage Manager Ruth Morgan

Assistant Stage Manager Daniel Precious

Music and soundscapes written, performed and produced by Guardians of Dalliance

Production credits

Picadilly
MRH Duplication
Radio Rentals
Paul Dipple
Mr Truman, Canley Ford service station
Eloise Clarke
Rebecca Marston
Poppy Woods

Sarah Woods
Writer

Trips is Sarah's third play for Birmingham Rep - previous ones being *Nervous Women* and *Bidding and Binding*. She has also been long associated with the Rep as resident tutor for the young writer's group. Other plays include *Two Faced* (Not the RSC Festival and Bridewell Theatre), and the hugely successful *Grace* (produced by Jade Theatre Company on tour, and nominated for the LWT Comedy Writing Award). She's also writing: a romantic musical comedy for Jade - *Life Candyfloss; On The Turn*, a play about ballroom dancing, for the National Theatre Studio and a new version of *Antigone* for Tag Theatre Co. Glasgow. *The Other Shore*, originally commissioned by the Soho Poly Theatre, has just received its premiere production at the Croydon Warehouse. Sarah is also a prolific writer of radio drama including her much praised radio trilogy *Hinterlands, Heartsong* and *A Lovesong for The Buses* (Prix Italia nominee), as well as the Classic Serial dramatisation of Radclyffe Hall's *The Well of Loneliness* (to be broadcast), Sarah is currently working on a new television series for Ragdoll Productions.

Sarah's work is *'frantic, fluid, tough, touching and very, very original'*
(Sarah Abdullah, *Time Out*, on Grace)

Lisa Ellis
Hayley

Trained: Central School of Speech and Drama
First appearance for Birmingham Repertory Theatre
Theatre: Kirsten and U/S Velvet in *Popcorn* (West End)
TV: *Devices and Desires*; *The Story Teller*
Radio: *Little Angels*

Karina Fernandez
Nik

Trained: Drama Centre
First appearance for Birmingham Repertory Theatre
Theatre: Lulu in *Shopping and Fucking* (Out Of Joint & Royal Court Tour); *Blue Heart* (Out of Joint & Royal Court).

Karen Tomlin
Ang

Trained: LAMDA
First appearance for Birmingham Repertory Theatre
Theatre: *Our Country's Good, Little Shop of Horrors* and Ella in *The Last Cuckoo* (Colchester Mercury); Coral in *Feasting On Air* (Paines Plough); Lucy in *The Beggar's Opera* (Belgrade Coventry); *Two Faced* (author Sarah Woods, The Bridewell Theatre); *Aladdin,* Ivy in *Beauty and The Beast* (Theatre Royal Stratford East); *Leave Taking* (National Theatre); Nerissa in *The Merchant of Venice* (Salisbury Playhouse); *The Supplients* (The Gate).
TV: *London's Burning* (ITV), *The Bill* (ITV); *Rides* (BBC); *McGuiver* (ABC); *Over the Rainbow* (Meridian); *Prime Suspect III* (Granada); *The Knock*; *Firm Friends II* (Zenith); *Casualty, Punt & Dennis* (BBC).
Film: *Diva - D.C* (NFTS)

Simeon Defoe
John

Trained: RADA
First appearance for Birmingham Repertory Theatre
Theatre: Cabaret Director in *Outside on the Street* (The Gate, London); Van Wart in *General From America*, William in *As You Like It* and Montieth in *Macbeth* (RSC); Corvino's Servant in *Volpone*, and GI in *The Women of Troy* (Royal National Theatre); Groneas in *The Broken Heart* (Lyric Studio Hammersmith); Tim in *Noises Off* and Gus in *The Dumb Waiter* (The Playhouse, Derby); Andrea in *The Life of Galileo* (Contact Theatre Manchester); *Jane Eyre*, (The Crucible, Sheffield).
TV: *The Bill, The Round Tower.*
Radio: *Lady Audeley's Secret.*

James Hillier
Dan

Trained: Graduated from RADA in 98, roles while there included Sloane in *Entertaining Mr Sloane*, Orlando in *As You Like It.*
First appearance for Birmingham Repertory Theatre
Theatre: Dorante in *The Bourgeois Gentilhomme* (Gatehouse)
TV: *An Unsuitable Job for A Woman* (ITV); *Great Expectations, Second Sight* (BBC)
Film: Jez in *Pipe Dreams* (Western Final)

Russell Mabey
Glen

Trained: Guildhall School of Music and Drama
First appearance for Birmingham Repertory Theatre
Theatre: *All In The Timing* (Tristan Bates Theatre); *The Man in Reader* (Oval Theatre); Franz Dreisseger in *Last Letters from Stalingrad* (Bridewell Theatre); Robert in *Reading Turgenev* (Meridian Theatre Co/Palace, Cork); Baecker in *The Weavers* (Gate Theatre); Lucky in *Waiting for Godot* (Portland Stage Co, USA); Usher in *The Fall of the House of Usher* (Cricklade Theatre).
TV: *Bugs* (Carnival); *The Bill* (Thames); *Road Rage* (Blue Heaven); *A Respectable Trade* (BBC TV); *Trial and Retribution* (YTV);
Film: *Spindrift* (BFI)

Guardians Of Dalliance

Guardians of Dalliance are a Midlands based dance outfit with a string of club hits behind them. As well as finishing off their first album (due for release early summer) they have recently had several tunes featured on programmes like *Eastenders* and BBC2's *Animal Zone*, and they are currently preparing for gigs at Glastonbury and The Solar Eclipse weekend in Cornwall.

Jeremy Raison
Director

Jeremy was Artistic Director of Chester Gateway Theatre from 1993 - 1997 for which he won The Stage/TMA Award for Outstanding Achievement in Regional Theatre.

Directing credits include: His adaptation, *Saki*, with Sir Dirk Bogarde (RNT); his original play *The Rain Gathering* with Ralph Fiennes (RNT Studio & Cottesloe, Traverse and winner of BBC/Radio 4 young playwright's competition); *Dead Dad Dog* with Robert Carlyle (Traverse Theatre & Tour), national tours of *Cat On A Hot Tin Roof* and *Three Steps to Heaven* (both nominated for Best Production Awards) *Macbeth* and *Betrayal* (Chester); and *Marivaux's Triumph of Love* (Chichester).

Other work includes directing more than thirty world premieres, including six of his own plays and his adaptation of *Charlie and the Chocolate Factory* which has been seen in the West End on numerous national tours and has been nominated as best children's show.

He is married with one daughter and lives in Glasgow.

Kit Surrey
Designer

Kit studied Stage Design at Wimbledon School of Art. He has worked extensively for the Royal Shakespeare Company designing some seventeen productions in Stratford and London, including *The Suicide*, Edward Bond's *Lear*, Howard Brenton's *The Churchill Play*, *Twelfth Night*, *Cymbeline*, *The Comedy of Errors*, *The Merchant of Venice* and *Much Ado about Nothing*, and was also RSC Associate Designer for the Warehouse Theatre. Recent designs include *The Servant*, the world premiere of Peter

Whelan's *Divine Right* (Birmingham Rep), *Blue Remembered Hills* (Sheffield Crucible), the British premiere of *Wolf - Ferrari's opera Il Campiello in London*, *The Turn Of the Screw* and the premiere of Richard Hurtford's *Bedevilled* (Theatre Royal York). He was the British Scenographic commissioner for the International Organisation of Scenographers (OISTAT) in Moscow (1981) and Berlin (1982). His landscape drawings have been widely exhibited in the West Country, where he has lived since 1974, and at the Cheltenham International Drawing Competition (1994).

Symon Harner
Lighting Designer

Lighting Designs include: For the Birmingham Repertory Theatre; The World Premieres of *The Tenant of Wildfell Hall* and *East Lynne, A Shaft of Sunlight* (For Tamasha Theatre Company), *Playing By The Rules* (also at the Drill Hall, London), *Turn of the Screw*, National Tours of *Metamorphosis* and *Kafka's Dick* (the latter being in collaboration with Lennie Tucker), *The Trial* (for The Mouse People) and *The Canal Ghost*.

For the Birmingham Rep Youth Workshop; *Pinocchio, The Threepenny Opera*, Tony Harrison's *'V'*, and *The Magic Toyshop* (also at the Edinburgh Festival in collaboration with Philip Swoffer.)

For Plymouth Theatre Royal; *Tales From the Vienna Woods* and *The Hired Man*. Most recently Symon designed the lighting for the *'Transmissions'* festival in The Door.

The Birmingham RepertoryTheatre Company
Introducing

The Door

Since it was founded in 1913 Birmingham Repertory Theatre Company has been a leading national company. Its programming has introduced a range of new and foreign plays to the British theatre repertoire, and it has been a springboard for many internationally famous actors, designers and directors.

Now the company can present classic, new and discovery plays on a scale appropriate to one of the largest acting spaces in Europe , as well as a consistent programme of new theatre in its studio, by some of the brightest contemporary talent To celebrate this, the space has a new name and a new look.

The Door's programme seeks to find a young and culturally diverse audience for the theatre, through the production of new work in an intimate, flexible space - work, that reflects, defines and enhances their experience of the world while introducing them to the possibilities of the medium.

Confidence: Jody Watson as Ella, Robin Pirongs as Ben
Photo: Tristram Kenton

Twins: Imelda Brown as Mimi and Anne White as Gigi
Photo: Tristram Kenton

Down Red Lane: Mathew Wait as Spider
Photo: Tristram Kenton

As the arts in Birmingham have grown in stature, with the opening of Symphony Hall, the achievements of the City of Birmingham Symphony Orchestra and the arrival of the Birmingham Royal Ballet so there has been massive investment in the resident theatre company.

'Birmingham...the workshop of the theatre world."
Michael Billington - The Guardian

New Work at Birmingham Repertory Theatre
- past, present and future

In recent years, Birmingham Repertory Theatre has produced a range of popular, award-winning and critically acclaimed new plays. These include *Divine Right* (1996), Peter Whelan's timely examination of the future of the British monarchy, Debbie Isitt's *Squealing Like a Pig* (1996), Nick Stafford's *The Whisper of Angels' Wings* (1997) and Ayub Khan-Din's *East is East* (1996), a co-production with Tamasha Theatre Company and the Royal Court Theatre, London.

In 1998, Bill Alexander's production of *Frozen* by Bryony Lavery, which starred Anita Dobson, Tom Georgeson and Josie Lawrence, was unaminously praised for its bravery, humanity and humour in exploring the intertwined experiences of a mother, the murderer of her daughter and the psychiatrist who treats him. *Frozen* went on to win the 1998 TMA Barclays Theatre Award for Best New Play.

In the Autumn, thanks to funding from the Arts Council's Stabilisation Scheme, we were able to start programming our former studio space – now renamed The Door – with a year round programme of new work. Opening with the appropriately named *Confidence* by Judy Upton and followed by Maureen Lawrence's *Twins* and Kate Dean's *Down Red Lane*, the theatre aims to provide a challenging, entertaining and diverse season of ten new plays, including two that tour to arts centres and community venues in the West Midlands.

In support of this work the theatre also runs an extensive education and development programme. Two of the plays in this season: Declan Croghan's

Confidence: Jody Watson as Ella, Robin Pirongs as Ben, Zoot Lynam as Dean.
Photo: Tristram Kenton

Paddy Englishman, Paddy Irishman and Paddy...? and *Trips* by Sarah Woods started life on the theatre's attachment scheme for writers. Beginning with just an outline or initial idea for a play, the writer works together with other professional practitioners including actors, directors and designers at appropriate stages throughout the writing process, with the ultimate goal a production of the play at this theatre.

Also in the Autumn, the Education and Literary Departments worked together to present *Transmissions*, a project in which young people from across the city of Birmingham, and from the ages of 7 - 25 wrote and presented their own plays with the support of professional playwrights, directors and actors.

If you would like more information on this or other aspects of our work, please contact us on

Tel: 0121 236 6771 x 2108/2109

Ben Payne
Literary Manager

The Birmingham Repertory Theatre gratefully acknowledges the support of the Sir Barry Jackson Trust in its new work development programme

From Page to Stage

An opportunity for students to participate in the process of putting on a season of new plays. Access to the country's most contemporary theatre writers, and a chance to work with directors, actors and qualified teachers in exploring a season of cutting edge theatre - Declan Croghan's PADDY IRISHMAN, PADDY ENGLISHMAN AND PADDY…?, TRIPS by Sarah Woods and NIGHTBUS by Peter Cann.

What's On Offer?

Workshops

On making block bookings, two workshops will be offered. The first involves an exploration of the content of the text; themes and structure etc. to be led by the Rep's Education Department and held at your college. The second will be run by a writer and the Rep's Associate Director Anthony Clark, and will explore ideas behind the writing and the process of producing the piece from page to stage. These second workshops will take place at the theatre.

After Darks

You can choose to come to the shows which are followed by an After Dark (although you are free to choose when you want to come). This is an opportunity to get the performer's perspective first hand, and to capitalise on that immediate response ensuring that your students get the most out of their time at the theatre.

Scripts

Scripts will be published for each play in a programme format. This provides an opportunity for further study of the text's form and content. Each student has their own copy of each play, at the equivalent of just £1.00. (These texts retail at £6.99).

Discounted Tickets

Tickets are available at the equivalent of just £3 per performance. With tickets normally at £9/£7, this represents a huge discount.

Unbeatable Value

Tickets for all three shows, scripts for each student, workshops with directors, writers and teachers and aftershow discussions with the company are included in the price. Stage to Page is a pro-active approach to serve mutual needs. An opportunity to tackle your curriculum in a unique, accessible way. Suitable for students of Culture, Theatre Arts, English etc. **The complete package works out at only £15** (minimum 15 students, no maximum).

What previous participants have said:
'My students don't usually have access to a professional director. It's brilliant'
'This has been the best part of the course for these students…I'm bowled over by the response. Terrific.'
'I really got to understand how complicated it is…I was much more into it because I'd read it…It was great'

For further details or to book please contact Rachel Gartside, Head of Education on 0121 236 6771

Transmissions: young playwrights

Communication, engagement and the start of something new

As Birmingham's only venue dedicated entirely to new writing, The Door is investing in writers of the future. In Autumn 1998 we launched the first part of our project with plays written by 7-25 year olds with staged readings and performances in our new writing house The Door. Short plays were developed in primary schools and through the Rep's young people's playwriting groups, led by professional writers and directors.

Those taking part in **Transmissions** explored writing, speaking, acting and reading their work with the guidance of professionals at every stage in the process. They developed their imaginative and technical skills in creating stories from action, speech and character.

In December the workshops culminated in a festival of performances. Examples of the extracts and scenes we presented include: *Wish you were here* by Modssor Rashid about a man's past returning to haunt him following his release from prison; Adam Godwin's *The Shop* which centred on the conflict of creativity and responsibility; and *Crossroads* by Sharlene Ferguson in which the friendship between two young women is placed on the line following a night on the town and an unexpected revelation. In all we presented twenty-eight pieces of writing over a two week period.

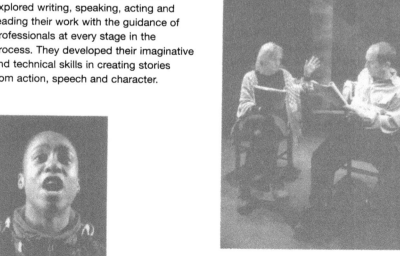

Photos: Alan Wood

There will be further **Transmissions** projects, including the continuation of the Rep's young playwright's group, which is now entering its third year. Many young playwrights from this group have gone on to develop their writing through higher education courses such as Theatre Arts or Drama at University.

'I learnt a lot about the hard work that is put into writing a play'
VINETA JAIN, SWANSHURST SCHOOL

'Helpful encouraging, insightful, inspiring'
TIM JEFFRIES, YOUNG WRITER

'Thank you for the chance to work with some inspiring young people'
MAYA CHOWDHRY, WRITER

'Young writers were exposed to a lot of talented professionals, inspired and encouraged to work and to believe in themselves. A lot of young people from the local community benefited.'
(THERSA HESKINS, FREELANCE DIRECTOR).

'The festival has given me practical tools to write my plays'
ADAM GODWIN, YOUNG WRITER

For more information please contact; Rachel Gartside / Liz Ingrams on 0121 236 6771 ext 2142/2104

What previous participants have said:

'Shy children came out of themselves and they all contributed to the script. Children and parents thoroughly enjoyed the whole experience'
TEACHER

First published in 1999 by Oberon Books Ltd.

(incorporating Absolute Classics)

521 Caledonian Road, London N7 9RH

Tel: 0171 607 3637 / Fax: 0171 607 3629

e-mail: oberon.books@btinternet.com

British Library Cataloguing-in-Publication-Data

A catalogue record for this book is available from the British Library.

ISBN 1 84002 110 1

Front cover photograph: Tom McShane

Typography: Richard Doust

For Crads

Notes on the text:

A forward slashmark / is used to indicate where characters speak at the same time as one another. This usually applies to immediately consecutive speeches unless otherwise stated in the stage directions.

Disclaimer: The text that follows is the one used at the beginning of rehearsals and may therefore differ from that used in performance.

TV credits:

Extracts from TV programmes were used in the first production of *Trips*. We would like to thank the following individuals and producers:

Celedor Productions for giving kind permission for us to use extracts from *Who Wants To Be A Millionaire*; Miss Cilla Black for kind permission to use extracts from LWT's *Blind Date*; Small Films for permission to use extracts from *Bagpuss*; Ragdoll productions for permission to use extracts from *Teletubbies* and Central TV for permission to use extracts from the news. Please note: in any future production of the play permission will need to be sought separately.

ACT ONE

Scene 1

ANG, heavily pregnant, sits in the lounge of the rented house. GLEN is in the kitchen, off to one side.

GLEN: Soy sauce.

ANG: No.

GLEN: Tomato puree.

ANG: No.

GLEN: Marmite.

ANG: A bit.

GLEN: Cumin.

ANG: What's the point asking me this every meal time?

GLEN: Garlic?

ANG: I don't want anything spicy.

GLEN: Come on.

ANG: I won't eat it.

GLEN: What about coriander?

ANG: We haven't got any.

He pops out of the kitchen.

GLEN: I'll go to the shop.

ANG: What's wrong with marmite?

He comes out of the kitchen.

GLEN: It's not Marmite.

ANG: It's like Marmite.

GLEN: It's yeast extract.

ANG: It's a very good source of iron, which should matter to you, unless you want me haemorrhaging all over the carpet.

GLEN: Marry me.

ANG: Before or after dinner?

GLEN: Whichever.

ANG: I'm too hungry to marry you now. I can't possibly get married 'til I've eaten enough to feed a family of four over Christmas and the New Year.

GLEN: After dinner. It won't be long.

ANG: I'm going to have some toast.

GLEN: Twenty minutes.

ANG gets up.

ANG: That's nineteen and a half minutes too long.

GLEN: You'll spoil your appetite.

ANG: Spoil – spoil my appetite – I can't dent it if I try.

She sits down again.

Ask me again.

GLEN: What about coriander?

ANG: No. Will you marry me?

GLEN: Yes.

I want to spend my life with you.

ANG: You already are.

GLEN: In front of the whole world.

ANG: So we can never escape.

GLEN: So we can never escape.

ANG: When?

He touches her bump.

GLEN: Pretty soon I thought.

ANG: Okay.

DAN enters from the hallway.

DAN: Something smells excellent.

He goes into the kitchen and starts helping himself.

GLEN: It's not ready yet.

DAN: Smells ready.

He comes to the door of the kitchen with a bowl of food.

GLEN: The beans aren't cooked.

DAN tastes it.

DAN: You're not wrong.

He pours it back into the saucepan.

What about garlic?

ANG: No.

DAN: Soy sauce?

GLEN: No.

DAN: Curry powder.

ANG & GLEN: No.

He pops his head into the room.

DAN: Bread anywhere?

ANG: In the bread bin.

DAN: Fuck me.

He presses play on the stereo in the lounge, then returns to the kitchen to make toast as NIK enters.

NIK: Something stinks.

GLEN: Thanks a lot.

DAN: It's not ready yet.

NIK: I mean in the hall.

ANG: It's Princess Anne.

HAYLEY comes in, wheels her bike across the front and off the other side.

NIK: Fucking stinks – like sour milk or something.

ANG: Nothing to do with me.

NIK: I nearly threw up.

ANG: I'm not touching it.

GLEN: It's Princess Anne.

HAYLEY enters and sits next to ANG.

HAYLEY: Something's rotting outside John's room.

AllbutH : It's Princess Anne.

HAYLEY: How are you?

ANG: Fine. Heavy.

HAYLEY touches ANG's bump.

HAYLEY: Tired?

GLEN: She's fine. I'm tired.

ANG: He's tired.

HAYLEY: Did you find anything?

ANG: That's why he's tired.

GLEN: I've got an interview.

HAYLEY: Excellent.

DAN comes out of the kitchen.

GLEN: At a twenty four hour garage. Doing the night shift.

DAN: Friends in high places. That's what we need. Smash the System from the inside.

HAYLEY: I'm being referred to the adjudication board.

ANG: What for?

HAYLEY: I got to the counter and they asked me how many jobs I'd applied for in the last two weeks.

NIK: They do that all the time.

HAYLEY: I said none.

DAN: What did you say that for?

HAYLEY: It's true. He said: why not? So I said I'd been decorating my room.

ANG: But you haven't.

HAYLEY: I didn't know what to say.

DAN: Say you've applied for every job advertised from here to Guatemala.

HAYLEY: But I haven't. I haven't seen anything. I said I'd been to the job centre.

GLEN: Have you?

HAYLEY: Yes. He said he'd refer it to the adjudication board who'll decide what sanctions to take – and I'll lose my money for between four weeks and six months.

DAN: Should've told them what they wanted to hear.

HAYLEY: I didn't want to lie.

NIK: You did lie.

HAYLEY: I didn't.

GLEN: You said you'd been decorating your room.

HAYLEY: I got in a tizzy.

NIK: That's a blatant lie.

HAYLEY: I felt stupid.

NIK: You haven't even hoovered.

GLEN: It won't be six months.

DAN: That depends.

HAYLEY: On what?

DAN: Whether they send someone to look at your room.

ANG: They won't do that.

JOHN enters with a massive old pram. As the scene continues, we see shots of everyone's rooms on the video. We don't know whose is whose, but sometimes we can guess.

DAN: They might.

GLEN: Dan.

JOHN: Glen.

HAYLEY: I'll have to decorate it.

ANG: You'd better apply for a few jobs.

JOHN: Ang.

DAN: They might find you a job as a painter and decorator.

DAN goes to check his toast, turns it over.

JOHN: This is for you.

ANG: Thanks John.

NIK: I had one of those when I was little.

HAYLEY: Why would someone chuck this?

NIK: I fell out of it.

GLEN: It's not exactly modern.

JOHN: It's chic.

NIK: It is chic.

GLEN: Won't be so good on the bus.

DAN: Pull it behind your bike.

ANG: Toast.

She goes to check the toast.

NIK: Bit high for a trailer.

JOHN: It says Style, it says Mother, it says Baby.

ANG looks out of the kitchen with margarine in one hand and a knife in the other.

NIK: It says: don't try and get me through a shop doorway.

ANG returns to the toast.

JOHN: It's not for shopping.

GLEN: Or round a corner.

JOHN: It's a perambulator.

GLEN: It's got fixed wheels.

JOHN: It's for perambulating.

ANG comes out of the kitchen with a plate of buttered toast. As she makes her way across the room, people take slices until there's none left for her.

NIK: You'll have to travel as the crow flies.

GLEN: (*To ANG.*) Are you going to tell them?

ANG: / You.

JOHN: Look at the suspension.

ANG: It's lovely, John.

GLEN: / You.

JOHN: You could sleep your way across a building site in that.

ANG: No.

GLEN: / All right.

JOHN: It's a tank. You're totally armoured.

GLEN: We're getting married.

HAYLEY: Congratulations.

JOHN: / Nice one.

NIK: Well done.

DAN: Why? You're already "married" – what do you need the state to endorse it / for?

GLEN: It's nothing to do with the state.

NIK: Why do you have to bring the state into everything?

ANG: We want to make our commitment public.

NIK: What's wrong with that?

HAYLEY: When?

ANG: Soon as we can, I suppose?

NIK: (*To DAN.*) What?

HAYLEY: What are you going to wear?

ANG: I don't know.

JOHN: Will there be food?

NIK: You've got to have a party.

ANG: Maybe.

JOHN wheels the pram further into the room.

JOHN: Here's to Glen and Ang and all who sail in her.

GLEN: Cheers, John.

JOHN shakes hands with GLEN.

DAN: Come out!

NIK: We're going to a club.

JOHN: House outing!

NIK: We're going dancing.

JOHN: Hayley?

HAYLEY isn't sure.

NIK: Come with us.

GLEN: What's all this crap?

ANG: I couldn't if I wanted to.

GLEN starts taking hubcaps out of the pram, JOHN takes them from him.

JOHN: They're mine.

NIK: Why not?

JOHN tries to hold more and more of them as GLEN unpacks them.

ANG: I'd be asleep before we got there.

NIK: This is some fucking sort of house.

DAN: Why don't we put on a big pan of cocoa and have done with it?

ANG: Hayley?

DAN: Why don't we all get our needlepoint out and crossstitch ourselves into the next century?

ANG: Take Glen.

DAN: Glen!

GLEN: They're filthy.

NIK: Come and celebrate.

ANG: Go on.

GLEN: All right.

DAN: That's a hubcap.

As DAN continues with his Crackerjack moment, NIK calls a cab.

/ And another hubcap. Remember, everything you can keep hold of you get to take home with you tonight. That's another hubcap. And another hubcap.

NIK: Can I book a car, please?

Fifteen minutes.

137 York Road. Nik. 'Bye.

GLEN: What do you want all these for?

JOHN: It's my new business.

ANG: You starting a business, John?

DAN: Another business?

JOHN: It's a great idea.

DAN: After you were so badly stung last time?

HAYLEY: Last time?

DAN puts the telly on and settles down with a rollie – the sound of the TV joins the music from the stereo.

JOHN: This is a really great idea.

He hunts around for a hammer.

HAYLEY: What happened last time?

JOHN: Wrong thought, wrong moment.

GLEN: He got a tip-off that the police were onto him.

You've never seen twenty eight –

JOHN: Twenty nine –

He finds a hammer in an unlikely place.

GLEN: Twenty nine dope plants move so fast. It was like a little piece of Columbia disappearing over the horizon.

JOHN bangs and bangs a hubcap with the hammer as hard as he can in an uncharacteristic burst of energy. Then he puts it on the coffee table in front of DAN.

JOHN: Dan?

All watch. JOHN gestures the hubcap. DAN looks vacant. JOHN takes his rollie, taps the ash from it into the hubcap and gives the rollie back to DAN.

GLEN: It works.

DAN picks up the hubcap and looks underneath.

NIK: It does work.

GLEN: But why John?

JOHN: I'm going to spray them.

ANG: Aerosol?

NIK: Woooh.

JOHN: Paint them.

The two sets of dialogue that follow happen simultaneously. ANG and HAYLEY talk about the pram as the others talk about hubcaps.

HAYLEY: Does the hood work?

As HAYLEY and ANG put the hood up and continue, the others start.

/ You could paint it.

ANG: I'll wash it and see how it comes up.

HAYLEY: I'll help.

ANG: Why don't you go out?

HAYLEY shakes her head.

ANG: Glen's going.

GLEN: What's your market?

JOHN: Thirty something. Professional. Big disposable income.

DAN: Low percentage of smokers.

JOHN: Have friends who smoke.

NIK: And children.

NIK comes over to ANG and HAYLEY, beginning her speech as JOHN continues.

JOHN: / Objet d'art.

DAN: How much?

JOHN: Twenty nine.

GLEN: Pounds?

JOHN: Twenty three – five.

DAN: I like it.

JOHN: Six. Twenty six.

GLEN: You do?

DAN: Nice and big. Room for a lot of smokes.

NIK: When my brother was born, nanny used to sit me on the top in a little chair, and no-one could see the baby so I got all the attention. You need a cat thing. A cat net.

ANG: Hayley says she's not going out.

NIK: Why not? And a parasol.

ANG: It's Winter.

NIK: A white parasol.

ANG: Go out and have some fun.

DAN: Where's the gear, John?

Silence. JOHN looks very worried for a moment.

NIK: John?

He looks into the middle distance.

GLEN: John?

JOHN: What?

DAN: The gear.

JOHN: What?

NIK: Where is it?

He looks round the room without moving.

JOHN: Did I have a coat?

GLEN: No, John.

He stands up, feels his pockets.

JOHN: Ooh.

DAN: Did you have a bag?

JOHN makes clicking noises with his mouth.

HAYLEY: Here's your bag.

He takes it, looks at it.

JOHN: Didn't take it with me.

He passes it to someone who passes it to HAYLEY, who puts it back.

NIK: Pockets.

He feels in his pockets, gives the contents to NIK and DAN as he does. We see these things on the video screen.

HAYLEY: You did get it?

JOHN: Get it?

NIK: Bus ticket.

GLEN: You did score?

DAN: Another bus ticket.

JOHN: Yeah – yeah.

NIK: Twenty three p.

JOHN: I had a smoke at Nibs'.

DAN: A dog end.

HAYLEY: Then what?

JOHN: Into town.

NIK: A match.

DAN: Four p.

NIK: Empty rizla packet.

Here's a bit of blow.

JOHN: Nice one.

He takes it.

I wondered where that got to.

He sits down.

I was up 'til half five this morning looking for that.

Anyone got any skins?

DAN: Sure.

He sits down and produces some.

NIK: The gear, John.

JOHN: What?

HAYLEY: You went into town.

GLEN: Where next?

JOHN: Went to The Copthorne.

DAN: The Copthorne?

ANG: What were you doing at The Copthorne?

DAN: Where next?

JOHN: Bus.

NIK: What number?

JOHN tries to remember.

JOHN: Sixty two – sixty three – sixty two – sixty three – sixty four.

DAN: Skip the bus.

JOHN: Skip: pram, hubcaps.

They all look at the hubcap ashtray. JOHN starts to skin-up again.

Top business idea. If ever I've had a top business idea, this is it, I mean –

DAN: (*Angry.*) John!

ANG produces a packet of B and H from the pram.

ANG: These yours, John?

JOHN: Tobacco, excellent.

They are passed to him.

It's only a matter of time.

HAYLEY: What?

JOHN: Before smoking comes in again.

He opens the packet.

It's the next big thing. There's a very big business idea in that.

Finds the gear in the packet.

I've got everyone's gear, by the way.

ANG: Where's Princess Anne?

As they continue, JOHN tries to sort the gear out.

DAN: She'll be at Balmoral.

GLEN: This time of year – you're joking.

NIK: She'll be at Buck House.

ANG: Has anyone seen her?

DAN: Not since she opened that Trout Farm in Sutton Colefield.

JOHN: What day is it?

ANG: Friday.

JOHN: Gatcombe, she'll have gone to Gatcombe.

HAYLEY: I saw her this morning.

ANG: Has she had anything to eat?

JOHN: We shared some porridge at about five this morning.

ANG: She's usually back by now.

HAYLEY: I wonder where she goes.

GLEN: Don't worry about it.

HAYLEY goes outside and shouts for her.

DAN: Do you think she worries about you?

ANG: It's just –

HAYLEY: (*Off.*) Princess Anne!

ANG: I want to lock up when you go / and I can't bare the thought of her sitting outside.

HAYLEY: (*Off.*) / Princess Anne! Princess!

DAN: She doesn't care.

ANG: Cold and hungry.

DAN: She's a Princess. She doesn't get cold and hungry.

NIK: She'll just go next door.

DAN: (*To JOHN.*) What did you get?

GLEN: Everyone knows her round here.

HAYLEY: (*Off.*) Coop-coop-coop-coop.

DAN: That's the beauty of being Royal.

NIK: Is it all right?

JOHN: Let's see.

HAYLEY re-enters.

NIK: Has anyone checked it out?

GLEN: I wonder / if I could get some.

JOHN: Nibs says it's Top Drawer. And some very tasty skunk.

DAN: I ordered two Es, a wrap and a pile of skunk.

All I've got so far is an empty B and H packet.

NIK: Think yourself lucky.

HAYLEY: (*To ANG.*) She'll come back.

JOHN: I don't need this.

GLEN: (*To ANG.*) Have you got any money.

ANG: I have to eat.

JOHN: How many do you want?

GLEN: (*To ANG.*) How many do I want?

DAN: Two. Two.

ANG speaks to HAYLEY.

ANG: Do you want to go out?

HAYLEY: No.

GLEN: Have you got any spare?

DAN: Hang on.

ANG: (*To GLEN.*) In my bag.

JOHN: You can only have one.

DAN: What?

NIK: Where's mine?

ANG: Do you want something?

HAYLEY: No.

NIK: Whose is this?

JOHN: Don't touch it.

ANG: Ask John. / Ask Nik.

HAYLEY: No. No.

ANG: I'll ask. Glen –

HAYLEY: No.

GLEN: Are you coming out?

JOHN: I want the money.

ANG: I'm so hungry.

NIK: So am I.

JOHN: I got what you told me to get.

ANG: Glen was making a stew.

NIK: Is it ready?

JOHN: You're all changing your minds.

NIK: Hayley?

HAYLEY: I'm all right.

NIK takes over the deal. As the others continue, ANG and GLEN talk.

ANG: / What's to go with this stew? Rice?

GLEN: I didn't do any rice.

NIK: Dan – two. Me – two. John –

JOHN: Three.

NIK: Two. Glen -

GLEN looks over.

JOHN: Glen didn't order. I know Glen didn't order.

NIK: One.

JOHN: He hasn't paid.

NIK chucks one to GLEN. ANG and GLEN continue as the others do.

GLEN: / There's bread.

ANG: Not any more. And there's no milk.

GLEN: I'll buy some.

JOHN: / None of you have paid.

NIK: Whizz. Whizz. Whizz. And a spare.

JOHN: Mine.

GLEN breaks off from ANG as the last wrap comes his way.

NIK: Glen.

He catches it.

GLEN: I'll buy you some milk.

DAN tests the whizz across his gums.

NIK: And skunk between four. How much is there?

JOHN: No. I'm not telling you. No.

NIK: How much do we owe you?

JOHN: (*Pointing at each of them as he says.*) Twenty eight, twenty eight, eighteen.

ANG: Does anyone want any food?

DAN: Bit late now, Ang.

GLEN: I'll leave it.

ANG: Hayley?

JOHN: Are you coming, Hayley?

DAN: If you stay in you'll have to talk about vaginal discharge all night.

ANG: How do you know?

JOHN: It's a house outing.

HAYLEY: Okay.

ANG: Are you eating, John?

ANG goes into the kitchen.

JOHN: I had a cheese and tomato bap and a cup of tea at The Copthorne.

NIK: They'd never let you in.

HAYLEY: Do they do baps?

JOHN: Outside.

GLEN: I thought they only did rolls.

JOHN: If you sit around outside, about half past six, a couple come with a shopping trolley and hand out tea and baps.

DAN: To who?

HAYLEY: To everyone?

JOHN: No. They select people.

GLEN: I think you'll find they're for the homeless, John.

ANG comes out of the kitchen with her food.

JOHN: They select me.

ANG: That's pretty low.

JOHN: What?

DAN: You're a scuz, John.

JOHN: Wha – what?

NIK: You aren't going out like that.

JOHN: What?

DAN: You'll have to get changed.

JOHN: I know.

NIK: You get changed, I'll sort the skunk.

JOHN: Right.

He goes to his room. As the others continue, we see him appear in his room. He undresses to baggy Y fronts and stands, vacant. Then he takes a pill. Then picks up other clothes from the floor and puts them on. Stands some more. Meanwhile, GLEN holds ANG's hands – they twist them around. As they continue, NIK and DAN fight: rolling around the floor, popping up behind the sofa. HAYLEY watches them. The two scenes run simultaneously. Just before the electricity goes, the video shot changes to show NIK's room: an electric bar fire glows orange, lighting up a very middle class room with scarves, ballet shoes and a violin.

GLEN: / You be all right?

ANG: Fine.

GLEN: Wish you were coming.

ANG: I don't.

I'd rather be in bed than taking class A drugs.

GLEN: I wish I wasn't going.

ANG: Am I showing my age?

GLEN: I won't be late.

ANG: Be late. We've got eighteen years of staying in ahead of us.

DAN and NIK run under ANG and GLEN.

DAN: Wrong. I'll sort the skunk.

He goes to grab it from her – she resists.

NIK: Fuck you.

DAN: Fuck you.

NIK: Fuck you.

DAN: Fuck you.

NIK: Fuck you.

DAN: Submit.

NIK: No.

DAN: Submit now or it'll be worse / for you.

NIK: You / submit.

DAN: Submit now or I'll hurt you and then you'll cry.

The two conversations end together as the electricity goes off: lights out, music and television off. The bar fire on the video fades very gradually. A moment.

ANG: I don't fucking believe it.

NIK: Put it on emergency.

HAYLEY: It was already on emergency.

DAN: Good job we're going out for the night.

ANG: If everyone gives me two quid –

DAN: I haven't got two quid spare.

NIK: Didn't I buy the token last time?

HAYLEY: I bought it last time.

DAN: Empty your pockets Nik, you rich cow.

NIK: Get lost.

ANG: Right.

DAN: Might be time to hawk the family silver.

GLEN: We can't leave you like this.

HAYLEY: I've got some money.

ANG: / No.

GLEN: Ang –

ANG: No.

NIK: (*To DAN.*) You had twenty quid off me yesterday.

DAN: True.

NIK: Didn't I buy the token the time before last?

ANG: I did.

GLEN: Ang paid for it and I went to the shop.

NIK: Only we haven't been around much this week.

NIK ducks out of the room.

DAN: We only got back the day before yesterday.

HAYLEY: I only put it in the day before yesterday.

ANG: Dan?

DAN: Some pay by cash in this world – I choose to pay in kind.

As the scene continues, we see NIK's hand appear around the door of her room and take her coat. There is just enough light from the fire to see her.

ANG: What?

DAN: I was happy to stand on top of Monsanto's marketing building naked if it protects biodiversity for future generations.

HAYLEY: How's it run out so quickly?

GLEN: Has anyone had a shower?

NIK enters wearing an industrial jacket with flourescent flashes on it.

ANG: I had a shower.

DAN: Action doesn't have a price tag.

HAYLEY: I watched Home and Away.

DAN: A simple thank-you will suffice.

JOHN enters, unseen.

ANG: Thanks, Dan.

DAN: Not a problem.

HAYLEY: It'd take an iron or an electric heater to use that much.

NIK: I don't use an iron.

GLEN goes to get a candle and matches.

ANG: (*Shouts.*) John!

JOHN: I only just got up.

GLEN: Where are you?

JOHN: Here.

GLEN: Where did you come from?

DAN: (*Deep TV announcer's voice.*) They came from Mars.

JOHN: Something stinks outside my room.

NIK: Something stinks in your room.

DAN: It's Princess Anne.

JOHN: Where?

ANG: It's cat shit.

JOHN: That's it.

DAN: Really needs clearing up.

ANG: I can't touch it.

JOHN: Not my cat.

ANG: It can kill the baby.

JOHN: Cat shit?

HAYLEY: Whose cat is it?

NIK: It's sort of a house cat.

JOHN: I don't like cats.

GLEN: Was it here when we moved in?

ANG: Nope.

NIK: It's everyone's.

HAYLEY: So it just wandered in?

NIK: Well. I found her. She found me.

JOHN: I hate this.

ANG: So do I.

JOHN: I hate this darkness imposed from the outside.

GLEN lights a candle.

GLEN: I think it's self-imposed.

DAN: Your shout, John.

JOHN: What?

DAN: Leccy token.

JOHN: Oh right.

ANG: It's not just up to John –

We hear the sound of a cab approaching on the PA. The image of the heater is flashed out by the cab headlights. The images continue as the scene does. The cab turns to face sideways on the screen and beeps its horn. It waits.

JOHN: How much do you want, Ang?

NIK: What do I need?

ANG: I'll go halves with you.

NIK: What do I need?

As DAN and NIK continue, the others start.

JOHN: I'll get it.

DAN: Pills. / Whizz. Chuddy.

ANG: Give us a fiver.

He does.

NIK: I haven't got any chuddy.

GLEN: Where are you putting your drugs?

DAN: Money. Fags. / Rizlas. Matches.

JOHN: In my sock.

NIK: Shoes – / where are my shoes.

GLEN: How stringent are the searches?

HAYLEY: Have you been there before?

JOHN: No.

NIK: Can anyone see my shoes?

JOHN: I can't even see my own hands.

DAN: Hayley, you're a girl, they'll never search you – put these down your knickers.

NIK: No.

GLEN: Don't, Hayley.

DAN: Someone put this plaster on me, then.

ANG does, the others are leaving.

GLEN: You got a job, Nik?

NIK: No.

GLEN: Only you're dressed like a security guard.

NIK: It's industrial chic.

DAN: Can we stop at the twenty four hour garage?

NIK: It's the new poverty chic.

His plaster comes unstuck and his drugs fall all over the floor.

Shit.

DAN and ANG grovel around by candlelight as the others exit.

GLEN: What about famine chic?

ANG: Here.

ANG gives DAN a tab.

JOHN: Hurricane chic is very now.

NIK: What about up your arse cheeks?

DAN: Where's me other E.

ANG: Is this it?

DAN: Cheers – this is a fucking lentil.

I don't fucking believe it.

The others are climbing into the cab.

ANG: There.

DAN: Where?

ANG: Next to the cigarette end.

DAN: Which one?

ANG: By the lump of hair.

DAN: Got it.

You're a hero.

He shoves everything down his sock.

ANG: Go on.

He hugs her.

You'll squash the baby.

The horn sounds as DAN exits. ANG stands. The cab lights flash across the screen again as it pulls away.

Fuck it.

The image of the cab fragments. ANG sits on the sofa. She starts to eat her cold meal.

ACT TWO

Scene 1

The club. Music plays and the video shows shots of a club and what might be on a club video. This is interrupted by other things which are indicated in the script. NIK and HAYLEY sit on the floor.

HAYLEY: Are you and Dan –

NIK: What?

HAYLEY: Going out.

NIK: No. Why?

HAYLEY: Only –

NIK: What?

> *As the scene continues, we see JOHN in the toilets, on video. He stands around a bit, then does some whizz, then stands about a bit more.*

HAYLEY: You're together a lot.

NIK: So are Andy Pandy and Teddy.

HAYLEY: Oh.

NIK: We're shagging.

HAYLEY: But it doesn't mean anything.

NIK: Of course it means something.

> *DAN and GLEN approach with bottles of water for everyone.*

DAN: What's that track?

HAYLEY: It means you're not Andy Pandy and Teddy, I suppose.

GLEN: It's Guardians of Dalliance.

HAYLEY: Have you taken yours?

GLEN: Not yet.

Dan?

Have you taken yours?

DAN: Not yet.

NIK: Aren't you doing one?

HAYLEY shakes her head.

GLEN: What are you going to do, are you going to take a whole one?

DAN: I dunno, I dunno what they're like.

GLEN: Shall we take half now and take the other half later if it's nice?

DAN: What if half isn't enough and when you take the other half it doesn't get you up?

NIK: What if it's horrible and mongy?

JOHN returns.

DAN: Do you know what these are like?

JOHN: No.

NIK: Have you taken yours?

JOHN: Yeah.

DAN: Are you getting anything?

JOHN: Yeah.

NIK: How do you feel?

JOHN: Great.

DAN takes his. NIK takes hers. GLEN takes half of his.

DAN: Who's here?

JOHN: Amp, Sinjun, Kate, Beany, Mez, Maz.

DAN: Maz?

GLEN: I thought she'd lost it?

JOHN: I guess she's found it again.

DAN: Unlikely.

JOHN: Depends where you look. I've found some incredible stuff whilst looking for something quite ordinary.

All right, Hayley.

HAYLEY: All right.

JOHN sniffs.

JOHN: Terrible cold.

GLEN: Is it contagious?

DAN: Fucking hope so.

HAYLEY and John begin over the others.

GLEN: / Have you had a line?

DAN: Not yet.

Have you?

GLEN: No. Are you going to?

DAN: I'm biding my time. Holding on to it for a bit.

GLEN: See if he can get his nose into someone else's.

DAN: Never know when it might come in handy.

NIK: What's up, Hayley?

JOHN: You look like you've lost a fiver and found the Lord Jesus.

HAYLEY: Do you think they will cut my benefit?

NIK: Forget it.

HAYLEY: I don't know what I'll do.

JOHN: I remember when I first signed on. Moved into a bedsit on High Street. I got £22.80 a week. I said I had asthma so I got a hoover. I got a heating allowance because it had high ceilings. Social security. I like that word.

NIK: Social?

JOHN: Security. I got cooker, a pair of curtains, a king-size duvet with a cover and pillows, pillowcases, sheets.

NIK: That was a long time ago, John.

JOHN: I've still got the bedding.

NIK: What about the hoover?

JOHN: I sold it on. It was a lifestyle thing.

HAYLEY: Are people selling stuff in here?

JOHN: What?

HAYLEY: Pills and stuff?

JOHN: Yeah.

HAYLEY: Do you know anyone?

JOHN: Daresay.

HAYLEY: Could you get me one?

JOHN: Daresay.

HAYLEY: How much?

She gets her purse out.

JOHN: All right, Hayley. Put your money away.

HAYLEY: I want to pay.

JOHN: Bit of discretion.

He rises, HAYLEY follows. JOHN salutes the others as they leave. Just before GLEN speaks, we see ANG flash up on the video screen. At first we can't tell it's her. The shot is of a twenty four hour garage. She buys electricity on a card from the attendant, through the hatch.

GLEN: I hope Ang is all right.

NIK: You need a mobile.

DAN: Why wouldn't she be?

NIK: She's fine. / You know she's fine.

DAN: She wants you to have a good night. Doesn't she?

GLEN: Yeah.

NIK: So have a good night.

DAN: It could be your last night of freedom.

The picture of ANG goes.

NIK: What's it like? Getting married.

DAN: He hasn't done it yet.

GLEN: It's like "yeah", it's like calm, it's like bubbles.

NIK: Bubbles?

DAN: Are you getting something?

GLEN: Very light and with a warmth and a solidity.

DAN: Like farting in the bath.

GLEN: Like yeah like –

DAN: Are you getting something?

NIK: Lemonade.

GLEN: But without the sugar and E numbers and shit.

DAN: Water.

NIK: Bubbles.

GLEN: Rising up but never bursting.

NIK: I'm getting something in my stomach.

GLEN: Fucking top.

DAN: I can feel a few murmurings.

GLEN: Fucking top tunes.

NIK exits.

DAN: I tell you what –

On the video we see a close-up of NIK's hands filling a water bottle in the toilets.

GLEN: Who's the DJ?

DAN: There's something.

GLEN: Fucking mental tunes, man.

DAN: Something's coming up.

DAN blows air out through his mouth as JOHN and HAYLEY return.

JOHN: Ah, look, it's Dan and Glen – Dan! Glen!

He hugs them.

GLEN: Fucking mental.

GLEN and JOHN shake hands. GLEN is grinning.

DAN: Excellent.

GLEN: Fucking wicked.

GLEN blows air out through his mouth.

JOHN: I really want you to have a good time, Hayley.

GLEN: Wicked night.

JOHN: I really want you to be happy.

GLEN blows air out through his mouth. We see an image of wrapped pink sweets swirling on the video for a few seconds.

HAYLEY: I am.

DAN: I love this moment.

JOHN: Are you?

DAN blows air out through his mouth again.

GLEN: Fucking wicked night.

HAYLEY: Yeah.

JOHN: Really happy.

NIK returns.

I'm really happy.

NIK: I want us all to dance.

JOHN: I want you to be really happy. Are you happy Dan?

DAN: Really happy, John.

Suddenly the lights go up in another part of the space to reveal ANG standing on a chair. She has just put the token in the electricity metre which lives in a little box. The TV and the music come on with the lights. The image of NIK's room comes up on the video as the heater starts to glow orange again. ANG stands on the chair for a moment, then gets down. Turns the music off, then the TV which delivers a final soundbite before it goes.

The video in the club space flashes up a surveillance camera-style shot of an empty corridor with a few steps in, leading from the dance space to the toilets. We hear the club music – a strong beat – and voices whooping and talking. The image changes to a close-up of the stairs. The music and voices are suddenly louder – and maybe slightly treated – as HAYLEY's feet rush down them. Now the shot is empty again, the music and voices back to normal. A moment. NIK enters, dragging DAN. Maybe it looks like they're going down the corridor the other way. Their voices rise out of the sounds we can already hear.

DAN: Where?

NIK: This way.

DAN: Where?

She stops, holds his hands.

NIK: What's going on?

DAN: A night out with friends.

The image on the video screen changes to that of the ladies toilets, empty. As NIK and DAN exit, the toilet door bangs open – the music and voices are loud as HAYLEY enters, then quieter again as the door shuts. HAYLEY can hardly stand. She crouches, her hands around her head, feels like she's spinning. The light is bright white. She grabs at a loo roll and holds it to her mouth – it reels out from her hand. She starts to chuck up into a basin. She's shaking, trying to wipe her mouth with the tissue and getting into a mess. The video shows the scene from different and strange vantage points – like a security camera. The footage is treated, moving at different speeds, missing out frames. It may mix from her

POV to ours, using computer-generated effects momentarily when we see things through her eyes. We hear lines from the scene sampled in the music which is building.

HAYLEY: What's going on?

In another space, ANG enters with a bowl and spoon. She starts tapping it.

ANG: Princess Anne?

She taps.

HAYLEY: Stop it.

ANG: Where are you?

ANG starts to exit as NIK enters without DAN.

NIK: Where are you?

HAYLEY: Where am I?

As the others continue, HAYLEY comes up close to the camera and looks out. DAN enters.

DAN: Come up close.

ANG enters in another different space, tapping the bowl.

HAYLEY: What have I done?

ANG: Princess Anne?

DAN: Go far away.

HAYLEY retreats from the screen.

HAYLEY: My hands.

We look at her shaking hands.

DAN: Come up close.

NIK: Stop it.

HAYLEY: Stop.

We see her pace round the room, strange angles: like the top back of her head.

ANG: Princess Anne.

HAYLEY: Help me.

NIK: Stop it.

NIK chases DAN off.

ANG: Over here.

HAYLEY: Where am I?

She looks round the toilet. ANG exits. A big bang as she shuts the back door and locks it. HAYLEY hears this.

HAYLEY: Princess Anne?

A moment. She rushes out of the loos. We see them empty. The image changes to ANG's back door from the inside as she draws two big bolts across. GLEN and JOHN enter.

JOHN: There's something about tonight. Something in the air. Like that Star Trek episode. The Omega Glory.

GLEN: Is it?

JOHN: William Shattner. Leonard Nimoy. Deforest Kelley. They find the USS Exeter, commanded by Ron Tracy. No damage to the vessel, but it's not responding.

GLEN: What do they do?

JOHN: Spock, Kirk, McCoy and Lieutenant Galway board and investigate.

DAN and NIK enter.

DAN: I can feel it.

JOHN: Something about tonight.

NIK: What?

JOHN: Something in the air.

We start to see HAYLEY in another space.

DAN: Go far away.

We see HAYLEY clearly, she has her back to a video screen.

HAYLEY: Princess Anne.

PRINCESS ANNE starts to appear on the video screen behind HAYLEY.

GLEN: What?

DAN: This is the most.

NIK: This is the most.

HAYLEY: Princess Anne.

We start to hear her purring as her image becomes clearer. She is huge.

DAN: Come up close.

NIK: You are the most.

HAYLEY: Princess.

She turns round and sees PRINCESS ANNE.

DAN: Go far away.

We leave the group and focus on HAYLEY.

PRINCESS ANNE: I love trout.

HAYLEY: I've not been very well.

PRINCESS ANNE: Don't you?

HAYLEY: Yes.

PRINCESS ANNE: Nobody knows how to cook a trout.

HAYLEY: I'm really ill.

PRINCESS ANNE: If Saddam Hussein destroyed the world tomorrow, the human race would vanish without ever having known the taste of trout.

HAYLEY: What do you think I should do?

PRINCESS ANNE: Gut it, scale it. Rinse a frying pan with flaming wine vinegar. Add a claret glass of olive oil / to three of water. A bouquet of thyme.

HAYLEY: I don't want to be here.

PRINCESS ANNE: Two crushed juniper berries, some pepper –

HAYLEY: I don't know what I'm doing here. I wish I hadn't come.

PRINCESS ANNE: Reduce it to one centimetre of fast boiling liquid and put your fine, fat trout gently in.

HAYLEY: I shouldn't have come.

PRINCESS ANNE: Do not turn it.

HAYLEY: I'm not part of this.

We hear the others approaching. They bring the music with them. They call HAYLEY.

PRINCESS ANNE: Cover it, boil for one minute, simmer for three, then serve.

HAYLEY: Take me home, Princess Anne.

Please.

PRINCESS ANNE starts to go.

PRINCESS ANNE: Now that's the sort of meal that makes me want to rub my arse up against someone's face.

HAYLEY: Please.

PRINCESS ANNE is gone.

DAN: All right, Hayley?

HAYLEY is devastated.

NIK: What's up with her?

DAN: I don't know.

GLEN: Hayley?

DAN gets the giggles.

HAYLEY: What's he laughing at?

GLEN: Don't know.

Everyone looks at DAN. He stifles his giggles.

NIK: All right, Hayley.

HAYLEY sits down. DAN giggles. JOHN giggles too. They can't stop.

HAYLEY: What are they laughing at?

NIK: They don't know.

HAYLEY puts her head in her hands. DAN and JOHN continue laughing. They eventually manage to stifle it.

NIK: Don't go to sleep, Hayley.

HAYLEY: I'm so tired.

NIK: Don't go to sleep.

HAYLEY: I'm so tired.

A moment.

NIK: Don't go to sleep.

HAYLEY: Mm.

NIK: Hayley?

HAYLEY: Mm.

NIK: Are you asleep?

Hayley? Hayley! Stand up!

HAYLEY: What?

NIK: Stand up, Hayley.

She stands up.

Look at me.

Don't go to sleep.

I'm being deadly serious.

HAYLEY: I'm not asleep.

She goes to sit down.

NIK: Don't sit down.

NIK starts to walk HAYLEY around.

HAYLEY: I don't want to make a fuss.

I want to be like you. Not you. All of you.

My heart's going to explode.

Where am I going?

NIK: For a walk.

HAYLEY: Is this happening to you?

NIK: What?

HAYLEY: This.

NIK: Yeah.

HAYLEY: Where am I going?

NIK: For a walk.

HAYLEY: Because I don't think it's happening to me.

HAYLEY grinds to a halt.

NIK: It is.

HAYLEY: This is your thing.

NIK gets HAYLEY to walk again.

All this walking and not sitting and not sleeping is your thing.

HAYLEY: Where am I going?

NIK: For a walk.

HAYLEY: Where?

NIK: We're here now.

They arrive. HAYLEY gets out of NIK's grasp.

HAYLEY: You're never in your room.

NIK: I am.

HAYLEY: The only time you go in your room is to get something out. Like a coat.

NIK: That's not true.

HAYLEY: When was the last time you were in your room?

NIK: Before we came out.

HAYLEY: Doing what?

NIK: Getting ready.

HAYLEY: What for?

NIK: To go out.

HAYLEY: Were you sitting down?

NIK: No.

HAYLEY: Are you tired?

NIK: No. Are you?

HAYLEY: No.

GLEN: What did she take?

JOHN: She just took one E.

GLEN: Who did she get it off?

JOHN: I got it for her.

NIK: Some likely lad.

JOHN: He's a nice person. He wouldn't sell me no
moody pills. He's not just a dealer. He parties.

GLEN: Did you have the same stuff?

JOHN: Just the one, to perk me up.

NIK: How do you feel?

JOHN: Bit edgy, bit –

He stretches his neck out of his collar.

You know. It's a perky little pill. Not so much in
the way of MDMA. Bit of acid, maybe. Bit of
Ketamin.

GLEN: And that's not a moody pill?

JOHN: Nah.

NIK: It's hardly fucking Farthing Wood, is it?

HAYLEY: There's nothing left.

NIK: Hayley?

GLEN: Fucking hell, John.

JOHN: What?

DAN: She'll be all right.

HAYLEY: Nothing left inside me.

DAN: All right Hayley?

HAYLEY sits down.

HAYLEY: I'm empty. You're all full.

GLEN: Should we take her home?

DAN: Nah.

HAYLEY: I threw my bones up.

JOHN: Oh God.

NIK: You didn't.

GLEN: I could phone Ang.

DAN: (*Quietly, in a silly voice.*) Ang.

NIK: She's been really sick.

DAN: That's a good sign. Get it out of her system.

NIK: Does she look like she's got it out of her system?

HAYLEY: My muscles are in a heap round my ankles.

NIK: They're not.

GLEN: Do you want to go home, Hayley?

HAYLEY doesn't move.

JOHN: It's all my fault.

NIK: It's not your fault.

HAYLEY: Where are my bones?

JOHN: She's going to die.

DAN: She's not going to die.

HAYLEY: I'm going to die.

GLEN: You're not – you're not going to die.

HAYLEY: I feel sick.

DAN: It's a rush.

NIK: You're really hot.

DAN: You're rushing.

HAYLEY: I'm so heavy.

DAN: Go with it. Don't resist.

HAYLEY: I can't breathe.

DAN: It'll take you somewhere beautiful. It's ecstasy. It's happiness. It's like coming continually.

He simulates the sound as HAYLEY panics.

HAYLEY: Where are my bones?

Someone get my bones.

She runs off. NIK goes after her. We hear them all around the space.

NIK: Hayley!

HAYLEY: Some fucker'll nick them.

NIK: Hayley!

JOHN: I can see what you were trying to get at there, Dan.

HAYLEY: Find my bones.

DAN: Yeah.

JOHN: Maybe it was the coming continually bit that –

DAN: Yeah.

Lights up on ANG. The others exit to look for HAYLEY.

NIK: Hayley!

ANG is hanging hand-washed second-hand baby clothes over a clothes horse.

ANG: I keep thinking: I know what you look like.

I've seen your face.

But I've never met you.

As ANG continues hanging the baby clothes out, we hear the voices of the others – off – around the space.

GLEN: Nik?

NIK: She's here. I've got her.

JOHN: All right, Hayley?

GLEN: Let's get her outside.

NIK: Dan –

ANG: You'd better not come early.

It's going to take the next two weeks to get this lot dry.

Eight babygrows. Three cardigans. One shawl. Six envelope neck vests.

Envelopes don't have necks.

Do envelopes have necks?

The fire door of the club opens to reveal HAYLEY. Behind her are the others. They're all lit from behind.

JOHN: Approaching planet Omega four, sir.

ANG: It's like a different world.

Wind blows their hair as they look out.

JOHN: Object ahead.

ANG: A whole different world.

HAYLEY: Wow.

JOHN: Another vessel in planet orbit, Captain.

Sounds start to create a soundscape.

Lieutenant's on alert.

HAYLEY: Have we done this before?

JOHN: Receiving no response to our signals.

GLEN: John?

JOHN: Lieutenant –

HAYLEY: I've done this before.

HAYLEY starts to come down the steps. The others follow.

JOHN: Have Mr Spock, Dr McCoy and Lieutenant Galway / report to the transporter room. We'll board and investigate.

GLEN: John?

The soundscape is building.

HAYLEY: I've had this moment before.

JOHN: Phasors on heavy stun.

NIK: Look at all the lights.

JOHN: Energise.

As they continue, JOHN is transported: he stands, scuttles across the stage and stands again – imagining he has appeared somewhere completely different. He looks around himself as if for the first time.

NIK: It's a completely different vibe out here.

JOHN: Just the uniforms left. As if they were in them when –

GLEN: What?

JOHN: Exactly.

HAYLEY: I'm so happy.

JOHN: When... what?

DAN: I know.

NIK: We're all in this together.

GLEN: What's going on here?

JOHN: Space: the final frontier. These are the voyagers of the Starship Enterprise. Mission: to explore strange new worlds, new life and new civilisations, where no man has gone before.

As NIK drains her water bottle, JOHN stops speaking and moves into the 'Star Trek' music, singing: aah – aah... The others continue.

DAN: There are no boundaries.

HAYLEY: I can do anything.

DAN: There are no frontiers.

HAYLEY: I can do anything.

JOHN: Jim –

DAN: It's a vision.

NIK: That's fucking beautiful.

NIK tries to open the fire door.

HAYLEY: I've never been this happy before.

NIK: Who shut the door?

I can't open the door.

DAN runs at it. The door won't open.

Someone's shut the door.

DAN kicks the door. From inside, someone bangs back.

GLEN: Someone's there.

DAN: Oy!

He bangs on the door.

Open the door.

NIK: Let me in!

Nothing.

GLEN: They've gone.

JOHN: The analysis of this so far is / potassium 35%, carbon 18%, phosphorus 1.0%, calcium 1.5%.

DAN: I don't believe it.

NIK: Great night.

DAN: Fucking wicked.

NIK: Fucking beautiful.

JOHN: Jim –

HAYLEY: I'm really thirsty.

JOHN: The crew didn't leave.

NIK starts to run off.

NIK: I'm going round the front.

JOHN: They're still here.

GLEN: They're not going to let you in.

HAYLEY: I'm really thirsty.

GLEN: Have some of mine.

GLEN gives HAYLEY his drink. As JOHN continues, HAYLEY drinks and drinks, draining GLEN's bottle. Everyone else's are already empty.

JOHN: These white crystals, that's what's left of the human body when you take the water away, which makes up 96% of our bodies.

DAN: I'm really thirsty.

JOHN: Without water, we're all just three or four pounds of chemicals.

NIK returns.

NIK: We've got to pay.

DAN puts his head in his hands.

What are we going to do for a drink?

DAN: Ring 999 and tell them we're dehydrating.

JOHN: Don't do that, Dan. They'll suss we're on one right away. "You're dead men – Don't go back to your own ship".

GLEN: All right, John?

JOHN: You have one chance –

GLEN: I'll phone Ang.

JOHN: Prepare to beam down to the planet surface.

DAN: Fuck me.

JOHN: Fast.

GLEN: She'll know what to do.

HAYLEY: Yeah.

NIK: Yeah.

DAN: We'll go to the fucking twenty four hour garage.

Images of Cornettos flash across the video screen.

NIK: Yeah.

HAYLEY: Yeah.

GLEN: Yeah.

PRINCESS ANNE enters: a four and a half foot tall fur fabric cat. She walks across the stage unnoticed.

DAN: Who wants what?

NIK: Strawberry Cornetto.

GLEN: Magnum.

DAN: White or brown.

GLEN: Brown.

PRINCESS ANNE exits.

JOHN: Princess Anne.

NIK: White – I want white.

GLEN: Where?

DAN: What would Princess Anne be doing here?

HAYLEY: Princess Anne?

NIK: Hayley?

JOHN: Maybe she came in the taxi.

DAN: She probably followed in her helicopter.

PRINCESS ANNE enters again and walks across.

JOHN: Perhaps she's come to warn us about something.

DAN: She's not fucking Lassie.

NIK: Crisps?

GLEN: Monster munch.

DAN: Flavour?

GLEN: Roast beef.

HAYLEY sees PRINCESS ANNE out of the corner of her eye as she exits.

DAN: She doesn't care about us.

NIK: Hayley?

JOHN: Princess Anne?

NIK: Do you want anything?

PRINCESS ANNE enters again, sits and cleans herself as they continue.

DAN: We're just commoners.

JOHN: No, Dan.

DAN: Every day we breathe the fumes from her shit – we're not even on first name terms.

JOHN: No, Dan.

DAN: This is my night off.

JOHN: Princess Anne's not like that.

DAN: Quavers.

HAYLEY wants to go to PRINCESS ANNE.

GLEN: They stick to your tongue.

DAN: You've got a point.

NIK: Monster Munch.

DAN: They're all the same.

HAYLEY begins to sidle over to PRINCESS ANNE.

JOHN: / Like when I got my money cut. I wept. And there was Princess Anne. "John", she said, "They're all fucking shit-faced wankers on this capitalist carbuncle that disappeared up it's own arse when the pagans were slaughtered by the Jesus freaks".

NIK: Hula Hoops. Snickers.

DAN: Mars Bar.

GLEN: Are you writing any of this down?

DAN: I thought you were.

GLEN: I haven't got any paper.

NIK: Nor me.

DAN: We'll have to memorise it.

They start to set off for the 24 hour garage.

GLEN: Princess Anne spoke to you?

HAYLEY: Yeah.

JOHN: She didn't have to say that.

HAYLEY reaches PRINCESS ANNE and puts her arms round her neck, buries her face in her fur. PRINCESS ANNE purrs.

DAN: She didn't say that.

JOHN: "You, John, you of them all understand".

They exit. We watch HAYLEY embracing PRINCESS ANNE. Then we hear the others again as they enter another part of the stage. JOHN walks slightly behind. He begins to speak as the others continue.

DAN: She's one of them. / He's lost the plot.

GLEN: Dan.

DAN: What's the plot, John – you've lost it?

NIK: Frazzles.

DAN: They don't exist any more.

GLEN: Like Top Cat.

DAN: (*Sings.*) Do-do-do-do-do.

JOHN: What's up, TC?

NIK: Is he black and white with a red nose?

GLEN: Top Cat?

DAN: (*Sings.*) Do-do-do-do-do.

GLEN: That was Sylvester.

DAN: He's the most

GLEN: Tip top –

DAN: Top Cat.

JOHN: "You John, of all of them, will be King when the honey of greed turns to tarmac in the fat necks of those who have said you are not actively seeking work".

As JOHN walks past a wheelie bin, he stops. The others continue.

Wow.

He looks in. His voice is echoed and amplified.

There's a whole world in here.

The others exit, still talking.

Scene 2

The video screen in the home space shows the electricity metre box. A hand – ANG's hand – appears and opens the door to reveal the electricity metre. We can hear it whirring as the numbers spin round. The hand disappears. ANG enters. She looks around for things that might be using electricity.

ANG: Television. Off. CD player. Off. Lamp. Off. Kettle. Not on. Cooker. Gas.

She puts her hands over her face. The whirring seems to get louder. She looks up, looks around the room.

Breville Snack and Sandwich Toaster? John's room. Video? Broken. Hoover? Would be nice.

She starts to exit.

Nik's room.

Scene 3

A wheelie bin. Puffs of smoke emerge from its lid. Then we hear JOHN speak, from inside. The sense of his speech is also carried by the images which flash, and play, on the video screen.

JOHN: Time to get up. Hat on. Nah – hat off. On the table. Where's my fucking hat? Hat. Where's my hat? Here. Put it on.

He sings.

"My hat. My hat. I found my hat. My hat – "

CHILDREN rush across the video, playing.

Yeah. Children. Ha – that girl, look. There's the girl. Fucking excellent.

A moment. The same video of CHILDREN plays.

Yeah. Children. Ha – that girl, look. There's the girl. Fucking excellent. And I'm like – fuck me... he-hey. It's the day for going round and round. I'm going round and round. In the house. Round and round the house. Outside. Round and round outside.

He laughs.

Go back inside. The hoover's scooting around like a fucking lunatic eating custard someone spilt on a chair like days ago – fucking eating my hat – my toast. Round and round the table. Round and round the bedroom.

What's that noise? U-oh. Outside. Go outside.

Something up in the sky. What? Lands right by us. Teddy bear in a merry go round. Does a dance. Flies away. Dance. We're dancing. Sunshine. Blue sky. All together. Dancing. Big hug.

VOICE OVER: Time for Tubby bye-bye.

JOHN: No – no –

The bin shakes and wobbles – the lid comes off and loads of smoke comes out.

VOICE OVER: Time for Tubby bye-bye.

No –

The bin falls over.

JOHN: U-oh.

VOICE OVER: No.

JOHN: Again – again!

Again – again!

Scene 4

HAYLEY sits, leaning against PRINCESS ANNE who is lying down.

PRINCESS ANNE: Sheba. Kit-e-Kat. Whiskers. Arthur's. Choosey. Felix. Paws. Happy Shopper. What was that cak you tried on me yesterday? I've been served some shit in my right Royal time, but that was the mad cow's bollocks.

You don't like cats, do you?

HAYLEY: I do.

PRINCESS ANNE: On Saturday, when no-one was about, you pushed me off the sofa, out of the patch of sun I'd been chasing round the room all morning so that you could sit in it. And when I tried to sit on your knee you crossed your legs and put the ashtray on them, even though you only smoke socially.

Why don't you go and find your friends?

HAYLEY: I don't know where they are.

PRINCESS ANNE: You'll find them.

HAYLEY: I don't mind it here with you, Princess Anne.

PRINCESS ANNE: I'm a cat.

HAYLEY: It's dark.

PRINCESS ANNE: You can't spend your whole life on my lap.

HAYLEY: I don't like the dark.

PRINCESS ANNE: You shouldn't come out at night.

A mouse scurries around on some steps in the corner of a video screen. HAYLEY doesn't notice.

HAYLEY: Bad things keep happening.

PRINCESS ANNE: Have you ever asked yourself why I'm here?

HAYLEY: Because I need you.

PRINCESS ANNE: At three in the morning.

HAYLEY: You're nocturnal.

PRINCESS ANNE: Or why I'm four and a half feet tall? Have you ever wondered why you find a four and a half foot tall yellow cat more comforting than your own friends?

Could you pass me that mouse.

HAYLEY: Where?

PRINCESS ANNE: There on the stair.

HAYLEY: Where on the stair?

PRINCESS ANNE: Right there.

JOHN is approaching.

JOHN: Again again –

PRINCESS ANNE: Go on.

JOHN laughs.

PRINCESS ANNE: You can't just sit and watch all your life.

HAYLEY: Let me stay with you.

PRINCESS ANNE is watching the mouse.

JOHN: The sun is setting in the sky.

PRINCESS ANNE: You have to catch the mouse some time.

JOHN: Teletubbies say –

PRINCESS ANNE: Here's John.

JOHN sees HAYLEY, but doesn't notice the cat.

JOHN: All right, Hayley.

He joins her, sitting against PRINCESS ANNE.

I thought you'd gone home. I should have known you hadn't. It wasn't finished.

HAYLEY: What?

JOHN: The vibe. I can feel it. We've got the same vibe.

PRINCESS ANNE gets up ands walks off. As a result, JOHN falls backwards – HAYLEY doesn't.

HAYLEY: Oh.

JOHN is puzzled but recovers himself.

JOHN: I know you. I feel like I really know you. It's spooky. You're young and I'm older.

You're a woman and I'm a man.

You've got brown hair and I've got red hair.

I've been thinking: maybe we should sleep together.

HAYLEY: Oh.

JOHN: Tonight.

HAYLEY: I really like you, John.

JOHN: I like you, Hayley.

HAYLEY: I really value our friendship.

JOHN: Just the same.

HAYLEY: I think sleeping together can really spoil a friendship.

JOHN: Do you?

HAYLEY: I couldn't bear it if our friendship got spoilt.

JOHN: Yeah.

Scene 5

ANG enters the sitting room of the house space with NIK's electric fire. ANG puts the fire down and gets the hammer. She hammers at NIK's fire until the element breaks. She sits back. As we continue to watch her, we start to hear the others.

NIK: Here comes –

DAN: Do-do-do-do-do-do-do-do-do, do-do-do-do-do-do-do –

GLEN: Pob.

ALL: No!

DAN: Do-do-do-do-do-do-do-do-do, do-do-do-do-do-do-do –

GLEN: No, I don't know.

NIK: Bod.

GLEN: Bod. Here comes Bod.

Who's Bod?

NIK & DAN: Who's Bod!

GLEN: Was he out of Heart to Heart?

NIK: No!

GLEN: Take Hart!

DAN: Po-po-po-pom, po-po-po-pom, po-po-po-pa-pa-pom, po-po-po pa-pa-pa-pa-pom.

NIK: PC Copper.

Scene 6

Gradually the focus changes to the group, outside the gates of a shopping centre. There is a TV shop and a security camera.

DAN: Di-di, di-di, di-di-di-di-di –

GLEN: Andy Pandy.

DAN: He was a mad fucker.

NIK: Andy Pandy was a girl.

DAN: Andy Pandy was a girl!

GLEN: He wore a blue suit.

NIK: Yeah but –

JOHN and HAYLEY enter, talking under the others.

GLEN: / Andy Pandy was a bloke.

NIK: No way.

DAN: What do you think he was called Andy for? Fucking Andrew Pandy.

GLEN: Andrew Pandrew. Andy to his mates.

JOHN: I wouldn't stop being your friend if it didn't work out.

HAYLEY: Even with the best of intentions –

JOHN: A one-off, then? Keep it casual.

HAYLEY: I don't know.

DAN: Bagpuss.

NIK: The most important.

Music from 'Bagpuss' joins the words.

GLEN: The most beautiful.

JOHN: The most magical.

HAYLEY: Saggy old cloth cat in the whole wide world.

DAN: Well now.

The doorbell in the home space sounds.

One day Emily found a thing and she brought it back to the shop –

We hear the doorbell at the house space. We see ANG.

ANG: Who is it?

DAN: And put it down in front of Bagpuss –

We hear knocking this time – we are moving over to the house space.

Who was in the shop window fast asleep as usual.

ANG: Glen?

DAN: But then Emily said some magic words.

Loud knocking.

Scene 7

We are focussed on the home space, ANG enters. The LANDLORD, played by Bob Warman, appears on the video screen. The LANDLORD and his speech are created from samples of Central News, cut together.

LANDLORD: Hello, good evening –

ANG: Hello. I wasn't expecting you. Do landlords normally call – ?

LANDLORD: In the early hours of the morning.

Now I wonder if you can help –

ANG: The rent's in the drawer.

LANDLORD: Let's take a look –

ANG gets it.

Happy days are here again!

She starts to count it out.

ANG: Twenty, forty, ninety –

She continues counting as they talk.

LANDLORD: It's make or break time.

ANG: It's all here.

LANDLORD: And we hope so.

ANG: Three hundred and twenty, three forty, sixty –

As ANG counts, the LANDLORD waits, looks serious, smiles, rolls his eyes, looks around. Looks at her, looks away.

Eighty, four hundred and ten, twenty, thirty, fifty, five hundred, five fifty, seventy. Eighty, ninety, ninety five. Six hundred. Six hundred and five, fifteen, twenty five, thirty, fifty. Fifty five.

There is some money missing.

LANDLORD: We've been here before, haven't we?

ANG: There was seven hundred here this morning.

LANDLORD: This is vitally important.

ANG: I know. There must be a good reason why it's not here.

LANDLORD: Yeah but what is it? Mm?

ANG: I don't know.

LANDLORD: But is it really good enough to row them out of trouble?

ANG: What sort of trouble?

LANDLORD: That's the hint, stay with it for the moment.

ANG: You're not going to chuck us out?

LANDLORD: But that's the answer isn't it?

ANG: You can't.

LANDLORD: It's harsh in a way because –

ANG: Because I'm going to have a baby. It's not me and Glen. We've always paid our rent. We haven't caused any trouble. Glen's looking for work now the baby's coming.

He's got an interview.

LANDLORD: Yes indeed.

ANG: At a twenty four hour garage.

LANDLORD: He makes me look good, I tell you.

ANG: I know you haven't been very happy about certain things. Like the rubbish piling up and us painting over your wallpaper. And I know the rent's very late, but I don't see why you want to chuck us out.

LANDLORD: Strange goings on –

ANG: What's strange? We're not strange. We're just six normal people who need somewhere to live.

LANDLORD: Stretching the imagination a little, I think.

He laughs

ANG: I know Dan and Nik can be a bit loud –

LANDLORD: At the risk of libelling the man, he's a nutter, isn't he?

ANG: Dan's not a nutter –

LANDLORD: They scare me to death, actually.

ANG: What about me and Glen?

LANDLORD: It's the old fashioned milk bars they want, all that frothy coffee?

ANG: We've got nowhere to go.

LANDLORD: Anyway, very good, thanks very much.

ANG: You've got to give us notice.

LANDLORD: Right –

ANG: You've got to give us two weeks notice.

LANDLORD: Yes indeed.

ANG: That's it is it?

LANDLORD: That's it.

ANG: Subject closed?

LANDLORD: For the moment – goodnight.

Scene 8

We see DAN. He is winding up to something. The night street sounds are becoming more threatening.

DAN: Bagpuss, dear Bagpuss, old fat, furry cat puss.

Wake up and look at this thing that I bring.

Wake up, be bright, be golden and light.

Bagpuss, O hear what I sing.

We hear BAGPUSS yawn. DAN laughs. PRINCESS ANNE walks across – maybe out of the theatre to front of house, leading the audience. Street sounds become music that takes us out into the interval.

ACT THREE

Scene 1

Back at the TV shop. DAN is right up to the security camera, clinging to the wall. He speaks in slow motion. GLEN and HAYLEY ignore him uncomfortably. NIK is used to him. JOHN wants to laugh.

DAN: Elephant scrotums.

A TV screen in the shop flashes on to show part of DAN's face – primarily his mouth.

Shite encrusted arse holes.

Another screen shows the same image.

Unlicked dog's bollocks.

Another screen shows the same image.

GLEN: Dan.

DAN: That's what you are.

HAYLEY: What if someone's watching?

JOHN doesn't find it funny anymore.

DAN: Some poor fuck who's been welfared back to slavery?

GLEN: I don't want any trouble.

DAN: (*To the camera.*) How do, mate?

JOHN and NIK begin to talk as DAN and GLEN continue.

JOHN: It's evidence. This is all evidence.

GLEN: I can't afford any trouble.

DAN: Can't afford it, Glen?

JOHN: I'm a law-abiding citizen.

GLEN: I'm going to have a kid.

NIK: Does that include the dealing, John?

DAN: Why don't you get yourself some nice carpet slippers?

GLEN: We're going to have a kid.

JOHN: (*To the camera.*) She's making that up.

DAN: Why don't you get yourself a cardigan with leather patches on the elbows?

NIK: Nice little earner on the side?

Why don't you get yourself some – a – why don't you get yourself – get a Remmington Fuzz-Away?

GLEN: I'm going to be someone's father.

HAYLEY: Why don't we get out of here?

DAN: You're just in your little corner. Going: "I don't do this. I don't do that". The politics of denial won't change anything.

GLEN: I'm not interested.

NIK: Not interested in what they're doing to our lives?

DAN: Not interested in the six lane toll-road they're building just over there?

JOHN: We're being watched.

NIK: Not interested in what they're doing to the planet?

DAN: Not interested in the genetically modified maize they're growing just over there –

JOHN: They're watching us.

DAN: And the biscuits and chocolate and baby milk full of genetically modified soya that no-one knows what effect it'll have on you?

JOHN: They'll send someone.

DAN: Or your children.

HAYLEY: Oh God.

DAN: Not interested in the sort of world your baby's going to grow up in? All the things it won't be able to do? All the people it won't be able to be. It's genetically altered soya today, but who knows what they'll be doing with their enzyme scissors tomorrow.

He goes to JOHN.

Snip, snip.

DNA cut, Sir? How does this yogurt weaver differ from a yogurt weaver? This is a yogurt weaver which has been grown using biotechnology to make it spam-resistant.

He goes up to the security camera again.

Are you listening? We've got to take action.

JOHN: I don't want you to do that, Dan.

DAN: It's what we do, not what we don't do. It's action, not sanctions.

JOHN: What's that?

HAYLEY: / What?

DAN: Doing, not doing without. Making not making do and mending.

JOHN: Over there.

GLEN: Fucking hell, what's going on?

DAN: It's now Glen. And now.

And now.

JOHN: Behind that wall.

DAN: And it's gone.

And that's gone.

And that.

GLEN: What is it?

DAN: So do it, Glen.

So do it.

He speaks to the security camera again.

No channel-hopping, now. No switching over to the pro-celebrity golf.

NIK: What's going on?

As the scene progresses, the TV and video screens show footage of everyone DAN's aiming his rant at. We also hear samples from them which build into the music.

GLEN: He's hit a wall. He's had too much whizz. / He thinks the place is crawling.

DAN: What's going on?

NIK: He's hit a wall. He's had too much whizz.

HAYLEY: What's going on?

JOHN: They're after me. They've got fucking guns and everything. Five of them. I saw five of them.

GLEN: Fucking hell what's going on?

JOHN: What's that?

Over there. Behind that wall. Just round the corner. They're going to fucking kill me.

GLEN: That's bad that is.

JOHN: You know what / they've got they've got these wave cameras.

HAYLEY: What? What've they got? / Wave cameras?

JOHN: Eight millimetre wave cameras that can see through your clothes and tell if you're carrying drugs and see you naked.

GLEN: Who are, John?

JOHN: MI6. Special branch. They've got our names.

DAN: They've got my name.

JOHN: We've got to get out of here.

DAN speaks to the camera.

DAN: (*As PROFESSOR YAFFLE.*) Nyaf, nyaf, nyaf, nyaf – well, I don't know, I really don't know.

NIK: Professor Yaffle!

DAN: It looks like – yes, that is a very dirty, very old planet.

NIK: He's a carved wooden book-end.

DAN: Yes. It's the planet earth.

JOHN: They're coming for us.

DAN: I'm not at all sure what we're supposed to do with it.

(*As the MICE.*) We will rub it we will scrub it, we will make it nice and new.

NIK joins in, also as the MICE, and the rhyme becomes a round. As they continue, we see ANG sitting in the home space with the pram. She has a bucket. She takes a cloth out of it and wrings it out. We see her on the video screen – live – as well as live in the home space.

We will do it, we'll go through it, that is what we'll do, do, do.

We will clean it, we will mend it, we will put it right, right, right.

Make you wish you'd never met us – we don't mind a fight, fight, fight.

NIK continues singing as DAN speaks.

JOHN: They've got guns, man. They're going to fucking shoot you down.

DAN: We will rub it.

GLEN: Shut up, Dan.

DAN: We will scrub it.

GLEN: Pack it in, Dan.

DAN: We will make it nice and new.

JOHN: Glen where's Ang?

GLEN: She's at home.

Lights down on ANG in the home space. She also disappears from the video screens, leaving one blank momentarily.

JOHN: Is she all right?

NIK: Of course she's all right.

DAN: This is the new party.

DAN speaks to the camera.

We'll practice self-rule. We'll decide what
matters, take part in our lives, control our own
lives.

JOHN: They've got my name.

DAN: We don't blindly obey, we resist.

JOHN: They've got my address.

DAN: It's our way.

JOHN: They've got my jacket. Where's my jacket?
I had it when I came out.

NIK: What do Special Branch want with your jacket?

JOHN: They're going to fuck up my housing benefit.

NIK: Why would they do that, John?

JOHN: They do that.

NIK: I know / they do that. I know exactly what
they do. We get pigged to fuck, me and Dan.

JOHN: They do that.

DAN: There is no plan.

NIK: They're not looking for you. What do they
want you for, John – getting out of bed?

JOHN: My thoughts.

DAN: There are no leaders.

JOHN: What's Dan doing?

DAN: No-one's telling us what to do.

NIK: You fucking yogurt weaver.

DAN: We feel it. We act. We direct our action.

NIK: You want to let your brain cool down.

DAN: Put me through to MI5, will you?

JOHN: Here's my drugs, here's my money. Look after them for us. I'm fucking going.

DAN: U-oh.

NIK: Where are you going to go, John?

JOHN: Stop shouting / will you stop shouting.

DAN: I'm not shouting.

GLEN: Don't go, John.

DAN: Listen.

NIK: We're all going to chill out.

DAN: I'm not shouting.

NIK: We're together. We're all together.

A moment. HAYLEY collapses.

GLEN: Shit.

DAN: Hayley?

NIK: Is she dead?

GLEN: I don't know.

DAN goes to her.

NIK: Has she got any breath?

DAN: I don't know.

NIK: Where's her pulse?

DAN: In her wrist / somewhere.

NIK: Feel it.

He does.

Can you feel anything?

DAN: No.

NIK: You must be doing it wrong. Do it again.

He does.

GLEN: Shall we call an ambulance?

DAN: No.

NIK: What if she's dead?

DAN: An ambulance won't help.

JOHN: Don't call an ambulance.

NIK: Oh God.

JOHN: Hayley?

DAN: She might come round in a minute.

NIK: Hayley!

JOHN: I hate that word.

NIK: What, might?

JOHN: No, minute.

GLEN: Shall I ring Ang?

DAN: Hayley.

JOHN: This is all my fault.

NIK: You could ring Ang.

GLEN: I'll ring Ang.

ANG, in the home space, begins to speak.

ANG: Wouldn't it be nice not to worry?

GLEN exits.

JOHN: I've done this.

DAN: Hayley?

The soundscape builds into music – maybe incorporating 'Bagpuss'.

ANG: Wouldn't it be so much easier to walk into a shop and buy washing liquid with optical whiteners.

The group are clustered around HAYLEY.

Wouldn't it be nice just to buy everything?

GLEN re-enters.

GLEN: Has anyone got ten p?

DAN: No.

JOHN: (*As PROFESSOR YAFFLE.*) Oh stop, stop, stop.

NIK: I might.

She looks in her purse.

JOHN: (*YAFFLE.*) You're all playing games again.

GLEN: It's not your fault, John.

NIK: Twenty?

JOHN: (*YAFFLE.*) I won't have anything more to do with you until you're properly serious.

DAN: Twenty.

ANG: Wouldn't it be nice not to live on the edge of things?

JOHN: (*YAFFLE.*) What a lot of bosh indeed.

NIK: Here's twenty.

She gives it to GLEN who exits.

ANG: Wouldn't it be nice to live slap bang in the middle of things?

JOHN: (*YAFFLE.*) I've never heard such nonsense.

DAN: Shut up, John.

JOHN: (*YAFFLE.*) Fiddlesticks and flapdoodle.

ANG: Slap bang in the middle of the six lane road.

JOHN: (*YAFFLE.*) It's a trick, a rotten trick.

DAN: Shall we sit her up or something?

NIK: I don't think we should move her.

JOHN starts to pace around, losing track of the others.

JOHN: (*YAFFLE.*) Oh ridiculous, ridiculous.

NIK: What are you doing?

ANG: Wouldn't it be nice to let go?

JOHN: (*YAFFLE.*) This is all getting very silly.

DAN: I'm trying to hear her breathe.

ANG: Wouldn't it be nice not to care?

JOHN: (*YAFFLE.*) This is all very unlikely.

Lights down on ANG.

NIK: I wish this wasn't happening.

DAN: Does she feel hot to you?

NIK: Quite hot.

What if she's dead?

DAN undoes her jacket.

DAN: Dead people are cold, Nik, very cold.

NIK: What if she's in a coma?

DAN: There's too much going on.

NIK moves away from HAYLEY.

NIK: I don't want to be here, Dan.

DAN goes towards NIK. Now that NIK, DAN and JOHN's focus is elsewhere, HAYLEY jumps up and runs off.

NIK: Dan?

DAN turns and walks away from NIK. As he does so, PRINCESS ANNE enters to stand behind NIK.

DAN: So Bagpuss placed the planet earth neatly in the corner of the window and left it there.

DAN gets his whizz out. JOHN notices and comes over.

PRINCESS ANNE: Don't you hate that?

NIK doesn't turn to look at PRINCESS ANNE, she keeps looking at DAN.

DAN: So that if the human race should happen to come past, they would see it.

PRINCESS ANNE: When you speak to someone and they pretend you're not there.

NIK turns to look at PRINCESS ANNE.

DAN: And come in to collect it.

JOHN: Is that your sherbert, Dan?

He has a dab of whizz.

PRINCESS ANNE: Or you're whipping round their legs and they make out they don't know what you want.

NIK turns to look at DAN again. DAN yawns.

PRINCESS ANNE: He'll shag you, but he'll never hold your hand in public.

JOHN: Dan?

DAN dabs at his sherbert.

PRINCESS ANNE: He'll never run to you through the winds of time.

DAN: And so their work was done.

JOHN: Is that your sherbert?

DAN: Yeah.

He has another dab.

PRINCESS ANNE: He'll never tell you your eyes are deep azure pools.

NIK looks at PRINCESS ANNE.

NIK: What?

JOHN: Could I have a little dab there, Dan?

PRINCESS ANNE: He'll shag you, you might even have his children, but he'll never pay their pocket money.

DAN: Sure.

JOHN sticks his whole finger in and takes a huge dab.

PRINCESS ANNE: Ciao.

NIK watches PRINCESS ANNE exit.

DAN: I'm going to the 24 hour. I need ice-cream.

He exits. When NIK turns round, DAN has gone.

NIK: Dan?

JOHN: Got any whizz, Nik?

GLEN enters.

GLEN: Did I just phone Ang?

JOHN: Couldn't say, mate.

GLEN: I had something to tell her. Nik gave me twenty p.

I haven't got it. I must've phoned her.

JOHN: What did she say?

GLEN: I can't remember.

JOHN: Got any whizz, Glen?

GLEN: I can't remember speaking to her.

NIK: Where's Dan gone?

JOHN: Twenty four hour garage.

GLEN: Where's Hayley?

A moment as they all look around.

Where is she?

NIK: You were with her, weren't you John?

JOHN: I dunno.

NIK: Maybe she's gone with Dan.

JOHN: Yeah.

GLEN: Is she all right?

NIK: Well she's not here.

JOHN: I think she went with Dan.

GLEN: I should've looked after her.

NIK: She's all right.

JOHN: Yeah.

NIK: She must be.

JOHN: I'm pretty sure she went with Dan.

GLEN: I can't do anything right.

NIK: You went to phone Ang. That's ok.

Lights up on ANG. We also see GLEN as she speaks.

ANG: He cares, your Dad. He really wants to do everything right.

He's just not that focussed.

But if he's not that focussed it's because there isn't one thing for him to focus on.

You show me a man who doesn't focus on one thing – he can't focus on the one thing that men do which is going away and coming back.

He is trying. He tries really hard.

He just forgets things sometimes.

And if he's forgets things it's only because he doesn't have thoughts like branches forking from the trunk of a tree.

You show me a man who does because all men have thoughts like one blade of grass, then another, then another.

It's hard being told you rule the world when you're not the ruling the world type.

GLEN: I'm going to phone Ang.

He exits.

ANG: And that there's no-one holding you back when you're not getting anywhere.

Lights down on her.

JOHN: They'll come back for us.

NIK: They won't. Once Dan went to the post office and left his giro in my room. He said it'd been stolen and got a new one. He never comes back for anything.

GLEN enters.

That's what he's about. Moving forward.

GLEN: Did I just phone Ang?

JOHN: Couldn't say, mate.

GLEN: I had something to tell her. I must've phoned her.

JOHN: What did she say?

NIK: Taking up the gauntlet.

GLEN: I can't remember.

NIK: Actually fighting for what he believes in, not just talking about it.

JOHN: He said something about ice-cream.

GLEN: I can't remember speaking to her.

NIK: That's what I'm about.

JOHN: Ice-cream?

NIK: Like china dogs.

A moment. JOHN and GLEN don't understand.

JOHN: Ice-cream?

GLEN: China dogs?

NIK: And crying clowns and pigs that look like Laurel and Hardy.

JOHN: I knew a pig who looked like Stan Laurel once. He nicked me / for psychic vandalism –

NIK: I mean pigs with snouts and curly tails that people try to tell you is art. That's not art. Crying clowns and china dogs aren't art.

GLEN: You look at china dogs.

NIK: I don't.

GLEN: Art is things you look at. Things you want to look at. A china dog on each side of the hearth.

NIK: Art is things you don't want to look at.

JOHN: A rotting sheep's carcass on either side of the hearth.

NIK: That's what my Mum says.

GLEN: I'm going to phone Ang.

GLEN exits.

NIK: She does interior decor.

JOHN: That's a good thought.

NIK: Amazing stuff. But she always says it's not true art.

GLEN enters. As the scene continues, images of NIK's world swirl around them. There are a few china dogs too, but they're outnumbered – almost hunted.

GLEN: Did I just phone Ang?

NIK: Mum really wants me to do an MA.

GLEN: I must've phoned her.

JOHN: In what?

NIK: Fine art.

GLEN: I can't remember speaking to her.

NIK: I really enjoyed my degree.

Mum and Dad feel maybe I need some more time.

GLEN: You know when you fill in your ticket at Argos?

NIK: No.

JOHN: Yeah.

GLEN: There's a bloke who goes off, fetches your china dogs and puts them on the shelves.

GLEN: That's my Dad.

JOHN: Really?

GLEN: That's what he does. Puts china dogs on shelves. Watch rugby, sleeps, watches snooker, mows the lawn if he has to.

Bought his own house in the end.

Put his own china dogs each side of the gas fire.

I used to think the worst thing that could ever happen to me was that I'd look at myself in the mirror and see my Dad looking back. Now that doesn't seem too bad.

JOHN: I never saw you as a china dogs man, Glen.

GLEN: I'm not, I just don't see why, after a hard day's work, a man / can't sit in a chair – or a woman – and look at a pair of china dogs.

JOHN: Or a woman. Sure.

NIK: I couldn't.

GLEN: If it makes him feel better.

JOHN: Sure thing.

GLEN: If it makes him feel good.

NIK: I couldn't fucking sit and look at a pair of china / fucking King George spaniels for one minute.

GLEN: And you'll never fucking have to.

JOHN: They're just a pair of china dogs.

NIK: / They're not –

GLEN: They're not just a pair of china dogs.

You can always go and do an MA. You can always get out of the room.

A helicopter on the video starts to circle them.

Can you 'copter me off? Daddy?

NIK: Yeah ha.

GLEN waves to it and shouts.

GLEN: Over here.

Quick!

NIK: / Yeah ha fucking ha fucking ha fucking ha.

GLEN: China dogs alert! I'm drowning in a sea of china bulldogs, airedales and cocker spaniels. They've eaten all my friends with their ceramic teeth and now they're starting on my Pantene Pro V!

As he continues, PRINCESS ANNE walks across the space. Only NIK sees her.

No, not my jodhpurs! Help me Daddy, please! Get your china tongues out of my Greek yogurt!

NIK watches PRINCESS ANNE go. The video changes to show ANG looking out of her bedroom window.

NIK: I'm going to find Dan.

She gets up and exits after PRINCESS ANNE.

JOHN: I think you've really upset her.

Glen?

I don't know if that was called for.

GLEN: No.

ANG walks away from the window.

I'm sorry about that, John.

Scene 2

Almost before scene three has ended, PRINCESS ANNE enters another space – it's the 24 hour garage, maybe on video. The forecourt is empty. HAYLEY is wrapped around the top of a telegraph pole nearby.

PRINCESS ANNE may stop and listen for a moment, or may leave immediately. HAYLEY doesn't speak directly to PRINCESS ANNE.

HAYLEY: I don't like trout. I've never even had it. I've only ever had cod and once I had haddock.

I don't like cats. If they were as big as dogs people would keep them in cages. I don't think they're mystical, I think they're a waste of Kit-e-Kat. I think Dan's right. I think we should act. All of us. Glen's a sound bloke but he's about as dynamic as a bar of soap. I don't know that I'd want his kid. If anyone's going to save the world and create a utopia Dan's the man, but it'll be a utopia with no electricity where someone's always just eaten the last slice of bread. I guess Nik's his bread.

As she continues, she stands up. During HAYLEY's next speech, NIK enters.

I don't really value John's friendship. I'd never sleep with someone who knows the 1986 'Countdown' final off by heart.

NIK sees HAYLEY.

NIK: Hayley!

HAYLEY: I couldn't sleep with someone who's underpants are older than I am.

NIK: What are you doing?

HAYLEY moves to walk across the telephone cable towards NIK.

HAYLEY: I'd never have an orgasm.

NIK: Don't move.

HAYLEY: And me?

NIK: Wait. Don't move.

HAYLEY : I can't just sit and watch all my life. I have to catch the mouse.

HAYLEY sets off across the cable.

NIK: Dan – she's going to kill herself – someone!

HAYLEY walks faultlessly across the wire.

Help me! Quickly!

Call the fire brigade. Glen. Someone.

HAYLEY gets to the other side and climbs down, reaching the bottom as John and DAN saunter on.

JOHN: I reckon interior decor's the way of the future. Computers – everyone working from home. I'll be laughing. Specialise in home–work environments.

Hayley.

HAYLEY: John.

JOHN: Nik.

NIK: Hayley –

GLEN enters.

GLEN: Did I just phone Ang?

NIK: Hayley.

GLEN: Did that just happen?

JOHN: Hayley –

NIK: Hayley walked across that telephone cable, /
in the middle of the air – walked across it. Fuck.

HAYLEY: I just –

JOHN: I've been really worried about you, Hayley.

NIK: Fuck.

GLEN: Did I just say I was going to phone Ang?

NIK: No-one's listening.

JOHN: I thought I'd killed you.

NIK: No-one ever listens to a word I say.

GLEN: Did I just go away and come back?

JOHN: I thought you were dead.

HAYLEY: I'm alive, John. I'm truly alive. I've
never felt so alive.

GLEN: Nik / did I just –

DAN: Give us a tenner, Nik.

JOHN: I wouldn't do anything to hurt you.

NIK: No.

DAN: What?

GLEN: What?

JOHN: You know that, don't you?

NIK: I know you don't want me for my mind.

JOHN: You know how I feel about you.

GLEN: Right –

GLEN exits.

NIK: I wouldn't mind if you wanted me for my body.

JOHN: You're a wonderful person.

NIK: But you don't. You want me for my money.

DAN: I don't.

JOHN: (*To HAYLEY.*) You're not full of any shit at all.

NIK: You do.

DAN: I want you for lots of things.

JOHN: You're empty of shit.

DAN: A tenner's just one of them.

NIK gives DAN a tenner.

JOHN: I just wanted you to be happy.

DAN kisses NIK.

HAYLEY: I am happy.

Glen enters.

DAN: I remember my first E.

JOHN: I just wanted everyone to be happy.

DAN: Now that was happiness.

HAYLEY: I'm really, really happy.

DAN: That was ecstacy.

As the others continue, NIK goes over to the garage booth.
We see the garage attendant. The others continue under NIK.

DAN: When every blade of grass in the universe
was in the right place.

JOHN: / Every blade of grass.

DAN: Every pane of glass.

JOHN: Every horse brass was in the right place.

DAN, GLEN and NIK look at him.

NIK: Strawberry Cornetto.

We hear CILLA BLACK from 'Blind Date'.

CILLA: (*Video.*) How do you like him?

NIK: And a Magnum, please.

CILLA: (*Video.*) What do you think?

Nik looks at DAN as CILLA BLACK flashes onto the screen.

Now did you get a bit of a fright there?

CHRIS TARRANT flashes onto the screen.

JOHN: Did I just say horse brass?

They nod.

CHRIS: (*Video.*) Eeeeeee!

JOHN reacts to him a little.

CILLA: (*Video.*) It's not a marriage made in heaven
for you both.

JOHN: I thought I'd got over that.

CHRIS: (*Video.*) John –

CILLA: (*Video.*) I hope you find the man you're looking for.

CHRIS: Hi, it's Chris Tarrant on ITV's Who Wants To Be A Millionaire.

JOHN comes over to the booth as NIK rejoins the others. They continue under JOHN and CHRIS TARRANT.

DAN: / What d'y get?

NIK: Strawberry Cornetto.

HAYLEY: Strawberry?

GLEN: What for?

DAN: What a mistake.

NIK: I love strawberry.

She starts to eat it.

GLEN: Cornettos aren't as good as they used to be.

JOHN: Who... Me, Chris. I do.

CHRIS: You're ready for this?

JOHN: I'm ready.

CHRIS: Ok. Let's play.

Which of these is yellow and pink: Battenburg cake, Tinky Winky, a turtle dove or the Queen's racing colours?

DAN: When every Cornetto in the world was in the right place.

JOHN: A – Battenburg cake.

DAN: They're not the same any more.

CHRIS: It's good. You've got a thousand pounds.

GLEN: E's certainly not as good as it used to be.

JOHN: The market's changed.

DAN: More and more people getting involved.

JOHN: More and more of a market force.

DAN: Everyone's taking it.

HAYLEY: My Mum's not.

DAN: Apart from your Mum.

JOHN: My olds aren't either.

GLEN: Nor mine.

DAN: Apart from your Mum, your olds, your olds – you know what I'm saying. Every pair of beer trousers and lager top. Everyone wants a fucking disco biscuit.

HAYLEY goes over to the garage attendant. The image becomes PRINCESS ANNE the cat – then the real PRINCESS ANNE – before returning to being the cat again.

And the profiteers spend the afternoon picking dirt out of their navels and the evening putting Dove stamps on it – if half of it's got any MDMA in it's purely accidental.

We need those testing booths like in Amsterdam.

HAYLEY returns to the group. The normal garage attendant returns momentarily.

GLEN: I really want to speak to Ang.

DAN: There should be one in every club.

JOHN: The fat cats want us all to be on Jealousy and Greed, but the people want Ecstacy.

DAN: The people want togetherness. The people want to be united.

NIK: The people want love.

Chris Tarrant appears on the screen again.

GLEN: Did I just speak to Ang?

CHRIS speaks to JOHN again.

CHRIS: Which country is home to the airline Qantas: Australia, Germany, France, or Qatar?

DAN: She got that right, Princess Di.

CHRIS: For two hundred quid.

JOHN goes to the garage attendant booth again.

DAN: She knew there was more to life than pomp. Than just circumstance.

JOHN: It's A – Australia.

CHRIS: You're right – it's the right answer, well done.

JOHN returns.

HAYLEY: I didn't know you were a Royalist, Dan.

DAN: Fucking not. Fucking hate the bastard lot of them, line them up against a wall and shoot the lot. Prince fucking Phillip first.

GLEN: Did I just speak to someone?

HAYLEY: United in what?

DAN: In our common vision.

HAYLEY: Of what?

GLEN: What did I just say?

We start to see CHARLIE MOUSE from Bagpuss.

DAN: Our common vision that we want there to be a common vision even if we don't know what that common vision is. We're living in the moment.

CHARLIE: Hello.

DAN goes to the garage attendant who is a MOUSE from Bagpuss.

GLEN: What moment?

MOUSE: Ooh – we are very fond of you.

JOHN: This moment.

GLEN: You're not in this moment.

MOUSE: We love you very much.

DAN: I'm in this moment.

NIK: Yeah / I'm in this moment.

HAYLEY: Yeah. I'm in this moment.

GLEN: You're not in any moment. You don't even know what day it is. You don't do anything. What have you done today?

JOHN: I put the kettle on.

GLEN: Only after waiting a couple of hours to see if anyone else'd do it.

JOHN: And when I put the kettle on I really put the kettle on with mind, body and spirit.

NIK: I'm with John on this.

GLEN: What if that's all he's done all day?

DAN returns to the group. The garage attendant is spinning now, changing at random.

NIK: Then he'll have done it well.

DAN: Better that than do everything badly.

GLEN: How many times do you watch Neighbours.

JOHN: A week?

GLEN: A day.

JOHN: Twice.

GLEN: And you're living in the when?

JOHN: That's recreation.

CHRIS TARRANT appears on the screen and continues under the others.

CHRIS: (*Video.*) You all right?

JOHN: Yeah.

NIK: You have to be mindful.

CHRIS: You calm?

JOHN: Yeah.

GLEN: I'm mindful of Ang and the baby and looking after them and giving them a good life.

NIK: You're not living in the moment, Glen.

GLEN: I am. All those things are happening in the moment: they're happening now.

DAN: You're living in moments to come.

NIK: You're not living in the now.

CHRIS: We've still got a million pounds waiting here.

DAN: You're living in the "what if" –

JOHN: And maybe.

NIK: When you take a step or light a cigarette –

DAN: Do it well.

GLEN moves over to the garage attendant who becomes
GLEN: the image of being stuck in a dead-end job. GLEN
the garage attendant looks out at us from every video screen.

GLEN: Pint of milk please, mate.

GLEN: (*On video.*) Skimmed, semi-skimmed or full
fat?

DAN: Every cigarette is different.

GLEN: Full fat, please.

DAN: Every potato is different.

GLEN: (*On video.*) That's thirty two pence please,
mate.

GLEN pays as NIK continues.

NIK: We should all be mindful.

DAN: And if we are mindful. And if we do things
well. Then things will be right.

ACT FOUR

Scene 1

Back at the rented house. ANG sits on the sofa with a hot water bottle, behind a large map of Great Britain. Maybe GLEN the 'garage attendant' watches her from a video screen. The trashed fire is on the floor. JOHN enters. He doesn't see ANG. He sits down at the other end of the sofa and puts the telly on: QVC shopping channel, 'Making Life Easier'. As he does so, GLEN disappears from the video screen.

JOHN: Multi-tray facility, I like that.

>It is an in-car system, Jilly. Very nice on a long journey.

>Lots of storage room.

ANG: You need a car, though, John.

>*JOHN jumps a mile.*

>It's all right. It's me.

>It's Ang.

JOHN: Ang. Where did you spring from?

ANG: Nowhere.

JOHN: Nowhere.

ANG: I've been here all along.

JOHN: That's the truest thing anyone's ever said about you. It's wise and it's honest which are both adjectives that sit well with you. You have been here all along, Ang. I realised that tonight.

>*He turns back to the telly.*

>Push button action, nice.

ANG: Is Glen coming home?

JOHN: Yeah, I should think so.

ANG: Did you have a good time?

JOHN: I don't know. I don't know if you would say that a good time was had by all. A good time was certainly had and I suppose it sort of moved through us, sometimes warming us with its rays, while at other times leaving us in its shadow.

Three quarters of stock gone already.

He whistles through his teeth.

ANG: Cheers, John.

Sound of DAN and NIK approaching – ANG standing now.

JOHN: Cheers.

DAN and NIK enter, sit on sofa.

NIK: What happened to my heater?

ANG: It's broken.

NIK: Oh.

JOHN: I didn't know you had a heater.

NIK: I don't use it.

ANG: You left it on. It must've overheated.

DAN: What's this shit, John?

JOHN: It's Make Life Easier with Jilly.

DAN: Have you bought anything?

JOHN: I just saw this incredible car storage system. / Very compact. No more mess on those long journeys.

ANG: Do you know where Glen is?

DAN: He's in a phone box.

NIK: Trying to phone you up.

ANG: On his own?

NIK: Hayley's with him.

ANG: Are they all right?

NIK: I think Glen wants to speak to you.

The phone rings – we see HAYLEY and GLEN in a phone box on video. ANG picks up the phone.

ANG: Hello?

GLEN: Ang?

HAYLEY: Who's that?

GLEN: Are you there?

HAYLEY: Is she there?

ANG: Are you all right?

GLEN: Is that you?

ANG: Where are you?

DAN: It's Glen.

GLEN: Am I speaking to you?

HAYLEY: / Who are you speaking to?

ANG: Glen?

GLEN: I'm speaking to Ang.

HAYLEY: Ang?

ANG: Is that Hayley?

GLEN: There's a lot going on here.

ANG: Come home.

GLEN: Ang?

HAYLEY: Glen.

GLEN: There's something I want to tell you.

ANG: What?

HAYLEY: What did she say?

ANG: Tell me when you get home.

DAN, NIK and JOHN begin.

GLEN: Yeah.

As ANG puts the phone down, GLEN and HAYLEY disappear from the video.

DAN: Christ, that's bad that is.

JOHN: These are special jewellery designs – that's the focus of this hour.

DAN: In a world cram-packed with tacky consumer durables, that is one tacky consumer durable too far.

JOHN: It's a clover and amethyst cluster set in genuine sterling silver.

DAN: It's a cluster of shite niblets held together by smeg.

JOHN: No, Dan, it's not.

DAN: I think you'll find it is.

ANG: They're coming home.

Now, do you want the good news or the bad news?

JOHN & DAN: / The good news.

NIK: The bad news.

JOHN & DAN: The / bad news.

NIK: Good news.

Bad news.

ANG: John, you owe me two pounds for electricity. Dan, you owe me sixteen.

DAN: Sixteen?

ANG: Nik, you owe me thirty one.

DAN whistles as the others speak.

JOHN: / Thirty one pounds?

NIK: What?

A moment.

DAN: What's the bad news?

ANG: We're being evicted in two weeks' time.

She looks at the TV.

Anti-static duster. That's quite useful. Is it? Maybe not.

They all look at the TV.

JOHN: It is useful. Instead of just moving dust around, the Once Over eliminates it.

NIK: I don't understand.

JOHN: As Jilly says, it's dead skin. Dust is dead skin.

DAN: How do you know?

ANG: The landlord came round for the rent.

JOHN: Doesn't bear thinking about.

NIK: The rent was in the drawer.

ANG: Not all of it.

NIK: My rent was in the drawer.

DAN: Not all of it.

ANG walks out.

I told you I was borrowing some.

NIK: You said you'd put it back.

DAN: I didn't know he'd come round tonight.

NIK: What are we going to do?

DAN: I had to pay John.

NIK: Where are we going to live?

DAN: In a tunnel.

JOHN: There's a room going at Nibs'.

DAN: Have they got cable?

JOHN: Check.

DAN: TV and building-up facilities in every room.

JOHN: Check.

DAN: And enough drugs moving through each week to kill half the voting public of Birmingham.

JOHN's watching the TV again.

JOHN: I think.

DAN: Everything a man could need without having to leave the comfort of his own bed.

JOHN: I could use one of those.

NIK: What for?

JOHN: You never know what's behind a wall.

If I drill through a pipe / I could have water everywhere.

DAN: You don't have a drill, John.

JOHN: If I drill through an electric cable it could be fatal.

JOHN gets up and goes to the phone.

513058.

DAN: John –

He rings QVC.

JOHN: You heard Jilly, whatever I'm doing at home –

NIK: Having a cup of tea.

JOHN: This'll stand me in good stead.

DAN: Skinning up.

JOHN: Fourteen fifty five – I've just saved my life.

It's 513058 – the stud, metal and voltage detector.

I don't have a credit card.

HAYLEY enters. Her scene with NIK and DAN continues with JOHN's monologue.

/ I don't have a cheque book. I really want one. I could get postal orders, but I'm out of cash 'til next week. No, I want to place an order now. You're going to sell out. You'll have sold out by next week. Could I speak to Jilly, please. I know she's on air. I can see she's on air. I do want to place an order – that's why I've phoned. If I could just speak to her. It's just – I could really do with one. It's for my business. I'm starting my own interior decor business.

HAYLEY: All right?

DAN: We're being evicted.

DAN starts to channel hop.

HAYLEY: What? When?

DAN: Week Monday.

NIK: Dan's going to live in a tunnel.

HAYLEY: Where?

DAN: Underneath the Ladypool Road.

HAYLEY: Why?

NIK: Someone didn't pay their rent.

DAN: Misunderstanding.

NIK: You said you'd put it back.

DAN: But did I say when?

HAYLEY: Where are we going to go?

JOHN puts the phone down.

NIK: John's sorted.

JOHN: I think I'll pop round there now.

NIK: It's half past five in the morning.

JOHN: You're right.

He takes out his whizz.

I'd better have another line.

Scene 2

GLEN and ANG's room. ANG is in bed. GLEN enters.

GLEN: Don't get up.

ANG: I can't sleep.

GLEN: I just want to see you.

ANG: I've been to the toilet about sixteen times in the last two hours. I might as well get up.

She sits up. GLEN gets into bed with his coat and shoes on, clutching a carrier bag.

ANG: Did you have a good time?

GLEN: Yeah.

ANG: Did you?

GLEN: Yeah.

ANG: The Landlord came round. He's not renewing our contract.

GLEN: Since when?

ANG: Since someone didn't pay their rent.

GLEN: Shit.

ANG: We're out in two weeks.

GLEN: Shit.

HAYLEY appears at the doorway.

ANG: Have you seen Princess Anne?

HAYLEY: No. Should I have done?

ANG: No.

HAYLEY: Have you?

ANG: I locked the door.

HAYLEY: Oh.

GLEN: She wasn't outside when we came in.

ANG: Did you have a good time?

HAYLEY: Yeah.

ANG: What did you do?

Neither GLEN nor HAYLEY can think what to say.

HAYLEY: We went to the 24 hour garage.

GLEN remembers the milk.

ANG: So did I. Which one?

HAYLEY: Deritend.

ANG: So did I. Come in.

HAYLEY: It's all right.

She goes. GLEN takes a pint of milk from his bag.

GLEN: I got your milk.

He bursts into tears. ANG takes the milk from him.

ANG: Glen? I thought you had a good time?

GLEN: No.

ANG: What's wrong?

GLEN: I missed you so much.

I'm so sorry.

ANG: What for?

GLEN: I'm a shit bloke.

ANG: You're not.

GLEN: I can't do anything right.

ANG: You got the milk.

GLEN: We won't even have a house to put it in, never mind a fridge.

ANG: We'll be all right. We'll move.

GLEN: Where to?

ANG shows him the map.

ANG: Here.

GLEN: What about the baby?

ANG: And the baby.

GLEN: This is my fault.

ANG: We need a new start.

GLEN: I thought I'd be doing better than this.

ANG: Selling conservatories?

GLEN: No –

ANG: Or making pies out of slaughter-house sweepings?

GLEN: No –

ANG: Managing a company that imports in-car storage systems from Taiwan?

GLEN: I thought I'd be doing something.

ANG: When I finished my degree, the sociology tutor asked us if we thought there was anything missing from the course. We said a few things and she said: work. There has been no mention of work. The work ethic. In the fifties, after the war, there was so much needed doing. Houses to build. There was loads of coal in the ground – there weren't enough people to dig it out.

Now people just work to produce crap. There's no sense of working to improve society's well-being. There's no need to work. What needs doing, Glen? These days. What really needs doing?

GLEN: The milk needs a fridge.

The baby needs a house.

ANG: I need another wee.

Scene 3

DAN is getting packets of crisps and chocolate bars out of his bag. They're covered in melted ice-cream. He starts to lick it. We also see HAYLEY outside the room.

NIK: You can't eat that.

It's all melted.

DAN: I'll unmelt it.

NIK: How?

DAN goes to the kitchen.

DAN: I'll put them in the freezer.

Freeze the whole bag and have a big fucking everything flavour Magnetto.

He returns.

NIK: You can't do that. It's dangerous.

You can't refreeze ice-cream.

I'm being serious.

DAN: Don't, Nik, it doesn't suit you.

NIK: Remember when Hayley was doing her nut and you said it was a rush?

DAN: It's a rush. You're rushing.

NIK: Go with it. Don't resist.

DAN: It'll take you somewhere beautiful.

NIK: It's ecstasy.

DAN: It's happiness.

NIK: Like coming continually.

She makes the sound as DAN continues.

DAN: Yeah. Yeah.

NIK: Excellent.

DAN: What a moment.

NIK: Yeah.

DAN: That was a moment.

Scene 4

JOHN comes out of his room and finds HAYLEY in the hall.

JOHN: All right, Hayley?

HAYLEY: Yeah.

JOHN: I'm just off to Nibs'.

Care to hop on board?

HAYLEY: No. Thanks.

JOHN: 2, 4, 6, 8 – who do we appreciate?

HAYLEY doesn't answer.

It can be anyone. You know, favourite football team or a person.

Catch you later, Hayley.

He opens the front door.

All right, Princess Anne?

He closes it behind him.

The End.